Cruising
to
Profits™

Volume 1 – Second Edition

Other publications by the author

"Impact of Passenger Airline Alliances on Air Cargo",
Journal of Air Transport Studies, 1995.

"Roots Air –Management Case Study for Graduate Studies",
R. Pilon / John Molson School of Business,
Concordia University, Montreal, 2001.

More information can be found at

www.cruising2profits.com

or

www.millavia.com

Cruising

to

Profits™

Transformational Strategies for Sustained Airline Profitability

Volume 1 – Second Edition

Ricardo Vincent Pilon

Curmill Aviation Publishers

Additional copies can be obtained from your local bookstore, online at www.cruising2profits.com or the publisher:

Curmill Aviation Publishers
5436 Royalmount
Montreal, QC H4P 1J7 CANADA
books@cruising2profits.com
info@cruising2profits.com

Cruising to Profits™
Copyright © 2014 by Ricardo Vincent Pilon
Hardcover: ISBN 978-0-9936889-0-4
e-Book: ISBN 978-0-9936889-1-1

Printed in the United States of America

Library and Archives Canada Cataloguing in Publication

Pilon, Ricardo Vincent, author
        Cruising to Profits: transformational strategies for sustained airline profitability / Ricardo Vincent Pilon

Includes bibliographical references.
Issues in print and electronic formats.
ISBN 978-0-9936889-0-4 (bound).—ISBN 978-0-9936889-1-1
        1. Airlines--Finance. 2. Airlines--Management. I. Pilon, Ricardo, author II. Title.

Volume 1 – Second Edition

Business Model, Process and Functional Integration

BeProFit (BPF) Business Transformation Framework Applied

Praise for Cruising to Profits

"Congratulations on writing this book. The message is so right and so clear. Sometimes organizations underestimate the importance of execution."
— Fariba Alamdari, VP Marketing and Value"
Boeing

"This book definitively got my attention."
— Allen B. Graham, President & CEO (Ret.)"
Air Transat

"Your work is good. Your approach can work provided the execution is managed properly."
— Nelson Gentiletti-
Chief Financial and Corporate Development Officer
Transcontinental

"This is a much-needed book and great topic. The airline industry is at a crossroads where this book adds great value."
— Chris Staab, Managing Partner-
Airline Information

CRUISING TO PROFITS
Transformational Strategies for Sustained Airline Profitability

"Your book is a very worthwhile effort. The topic is obviously important and you clearly show that you are getting into the details of strategy implementation and some of the real problems of converting business models and strategic intent into actions. I like the fact that you also advance tools and techniques, which of course is what many managers are after these days."

— Dr. William D. Taylor, Professor Emeritus
John Molson School of Business

"Our client projects have demonstrated the tremendous power of prescriptive analytics and customer-centric personalization. This book lays a solid foundation for the evolution of business management in the airline business."

– Michael Foliot, President & CEO
TDT Business Solutions & Analytics.

Dedication

To all people that embrace and celebrate life, love, health and friendship, ...and aviation!

CRUISING TO PROFITS
Transformational Strategies for Sustained Airline Profitability

Table of Contents

CRUISING TO PROFITS
Transformational Strategies for Sustained Airline Profitability

CRUISING TO PROFITS

Transformational Strategies for Sustained Airline Profitability

CRUISING TO PROFITS

Transformational Strategies for Sustained Airline Profitability

Preface

On January 1, 2014 and the airline industry is celebrating its first centennial, the 100th anniversary of the first commercial-airline flight, which took place between St. Petersburg and Tampa, Florida[i]. Fast-forward to today, and the world's largest ever airline is in the making with the proposed merger between US Airways and American Airlines, creating an airline company with 110,000 employees, more than 1500 aircraft, 6,700 daily departures, and 336 destinations in 56 countries. The industry overall is generating a whopping USD 711 billion in revenues, transporting just over three billion passengers per year.

While for some people aviation appears to be so common and interwoven in our daily lives, like it has always existed, the airline business is comparatively speaking a young industry that arguably has only started to evolve. Even so, due to the visibility the industry tends to face, many are aware of its cyclical nature, with oftentimes widely reported severe losses or revenue upswings.

CRUISING TO PROFITS
Transformational Strategies for Sustained Airline Profitability

Although many industries experience repeated cycles, airlines can report mammoth losses in one year, then exhibit hundreds of millions of profits in the next, owing to fluctuating exchange rates, jet aviation A-1 fuel prices, union strikes, natural disasters, and overall decline in business volumes. This only demonstrates that slim margins typify the business. A one percent increase in yield can lead to profits due to the sheer size of current operations. The industry is unfortunately connected to overall yields that have been on a steady decline since the late 1970s. This is arguably related to structural overcapacity but also to an underscoring and troubling tendency of the travelling public to perceive air transportation as a commodity. Today's paradox is that customers trust airlines with their lives, but they do not trust them with their dollars. One may thus conclude that the willingness to pay has corroded, or that we have tapped into market segments that are just not commercially viable and do not belong within scope or scale.

For instance, if all airlines combined had been able to charge between USD 2 to 4 per passenger more, the global airline industry would have been profitable during most of the recent troughs and downturns since September 11, 2001. Some contend that the industry appears to have a severe pricing competency problem. Future efforts should be directed toward correcting this fundamental quandary.

"It is still a very tough business"
— Tony Tyler, Director General and CEO, IATA.

While it is a fact that airlines have spent a great deal of effort and have invested into the area of revenue management ever since the early 1980s, this discipline has typically used artificial market segmentation, leaving few in a position to understand the complex fare structures and associated service levels that so well typified the 1990s. Current revenue management also relies on business assumptions that are fundamentally flawed and become invalid as soon as underlying circumstances or business models change.

From a marketing point of view, the airlines have tended to over-promise and under-deliver on passenger experience. While we see — on TV and in print — airline advertisements of passengers being spoiled in spacious economy cabins as if one were staying at a luxury hotel, the reality and experience is much different in the cramped cabins and narrow seats on board, where "service" is delivered according to a mass-delivery timed program. Due to this type of "mass transportation," one endures an impersonalized treatment. This is not a true service industry.

"There is room for more than two models in the industry landscape"
— Dave Barger, CEO, jetBlue

The above leads us to assume that there exists an acute incongruity between passenger needs and available service products. Passengers do not consume air travel. The latter is a means to an end, or part of a larger need from which this derived demand occurs, while most airlines continue to concentrate on improvements of "in-flight." Conversely, the demand for air travel and its associated needs vary greatly from each customer to the next. However, little has so far been done to consider each individual, and to provide a truly personalized offer as part of each person's purpose of travel. And while there is a movement and a need to move to retail enablement, many obstacles to this still exist, notably current operating models that include barriers that are far beyond any airline's hegemony.

In the end, there is no true economic recovery in our industry today, and improvement in performance will come only through structural change, both internal and external.

"With collective will and vision, the industry can create a new "shared template for modern [air] services… [….]".
— Robert Milton, Fmr. Chairman, President & CEO, ACE Aviation Holdings.

It is often said that there is a clear distinction between leadership and management. *Cruising to Profits* is the first part of a leadership initiative aimed at contributing to restoring the core of airline profitability, an initiative that will provide innovative perspectives on airline management today as well as management opportunities going forward. As a result, this book distinguishes between industry-level strategy and company-level strategy, as some of the challenges to overcome require industry leadership, as they are fundamental and related to root causes of the woes of airline profitability.

This book was written as a means to compile all practitioner and consulting work we have performed in the airline business and to structure the gained expertise and experience along with our academic work and achievements in the industry. It is aimed to question key established practices, in order to constructively propose future ones. Subsequent work will provide further, detailed and practical guidelines and toolkits that airlines will be able to use in their organizations to align business functions and integrate business processes in order to support their defined business model (called "**BeProFit**" – **BPF**). In addition, our book will allow airlines to recognize that each task and activity in the organization could have a role in identifying value by embedding value-based strategy formulation in day-to-day processes. The described approach is a departure from conventional airline planning but a necessary means to address the fundamental challenges that plague our industry.

Also, this book attempts to explore a more holistic approach to airline strategy and marketing, by reflecting on today's business models, by identifying key attention areas and pressure points, and by proposing a new management approach as part of a more holistic view of the air transport industry. Furthermore, due to the fact that re-inventing business models today can only be achieved by questioning current practices and related information technology; a few chapters are dedicated to address future business-technology needs.

Finally, this book is not about flying, aircraft, or the environmental debate the industry is getting tangled into. *Cruising to Profits* is the book that sets the tone for its sequels, which offer toolkits based on the management approaches described in this book. We did not intend to cover all aspects and degrees of detail in a single publication.

Chapter 1
Introduction

Aviation evokes emotions. It triggers both positive and negative emotions and feelings. Aviation was once glamour and grandness reserved for the select few, simply due to the costs of providing air transport service in its early pioneering days. But the airline business has evolved much differently than suggested decades ago.

Airplanes carry people through the skies that surround our globe and have as such fascinated many, if not most, with the principles of flight, the wonders of the world, the various civilizations occupying this world, and the ability to witness all this independently of which place one calls home. Aviation inherently involves transportation, but being transported means something more than being taken from point A to B and this emotional component is often overlooked and not fully exploited in airline marketing and business models today.

At a more fundamental level, the experience of air transportation is important but should be considered a subset of the overall purpose of travel. It is this division that spells the difference between profitability and production for market share. I refer to this as tubular thinking (as in the aircraft "tube"), a framed or limited view of aviation that practically assumes that demand for air transport is a consumption good and that the sole purpose is the travel itself that is being "consumed." But it is a means to an end.

One can take great inspiration from the blue sky thinking in terms of air transportation, but intriguingly none of this is taking a deeper look at the underlying fundamental financial issues around the airline business in its purest economical form. That is, a proper and healthy rate of return to shareholders and all stakeholders that provided the financial infrastructure to conduct business and fly airplanes around.

For instance, futurologists and aircraft manufacturers Boeing and Airbus have dedicated teams that study new ways and forms of future air travel, often with the help of aeronautical engineering departments of recognized institutes and universities like Embry-Riddle and Cranfield University. The blue sky thinking they are permitted to do is leading toward changes in fuselage shapes, tail planes, but also to transparent cabins and intelligent seats. And the supersonic business jets are also making a return.

Airbus' Future Concept Plane is touting aircraft that allow the placing of carry-on bags on delivery belts overhead so that passengers find their bags overhead when they get to their seats. Bunk beds (allowing every passenger aisle access) in business class have been studied, as well as seats that adapt humidity around a person's body and absorb excess energy for use on board to power aircraft components. There also appears to be a movement of creating cabins on board not based on pure legroom and IFE but in-flight activities (rest, gaming, dining, business and technology), so that passengers can book themselves into the cabin that will accommodate what they intend to do onboard, irrespective of day or night flight times. Some of it is true sci-fi sounding future "Dreamliner," but it does help shape debates on passenger behavior and may ultimately allow us to bring the perceived value of air transportation more in line with the cost of providing the services. Today, as an industry, we have not been capable of attaining this across all customer segments and we therefore require sub-segments to subsidize the air fares of others. It can be seen as *the social face* of air transport in light of facilitating people and travelers to meet other people around the globe to do what it is they wish to do.

Ultimately, the scramble to enhance space utilization, comfort and passenger convenience is already creating a competitive frenzy among international carriers, driven by innovative carriers such as Air New Zealand and Virgin Atlantic Airways, but being in the end still a reflection of the tubular view of the industry.

Like many involved in the airline industry, a lot of people are fascinated by or obsessed with aircraft, and airline managers and marketers themselves often focus on the aircraft and cabin interior components in their marketing campaigns. As said, I refer to this as tubular thinking, a framed or limited view of aviation that practically assumes that demand for air transport is a consumption good and that the sole purpose is the travel itself that is being "consumed". However, short of a select few airline enthusiasts, air transport is a means to an end. In economic terms, air transport is a derived demand, driven by a larger and more complex type of demand. There is, however, a persistent tendency to overlook this fundamental characteristic of the airline business, and this tendency is arguably connected to one of the structural pitfalls of airline business models. But economic activity remains the key driver to underlying demand with supply, determined by net new deliveries and deployment decisions.

Another dichotomy of the demand for air travel and of air transport services is that while aircraft would appear to represent ultimate mobility, the airline business is in fact a very immobile industry. Safety regulations aside, the business is plagued with restrictive legislation on traffic rights and with union-driven work rules that effectively render the airline business inflexible and make it difficult for everyone involved to deal with shifting economic realities. To some extent, a lot of duplication of effort (i.e., equipment, services, etc.) exists in order to overcome such restrictions, although marketing arrangements and deeper relationships, such as alliances and joint ventures to circumvent restrictions, can also act to rationalize the amount of equipment deployment and production.

It is very important to conceptualize new business models that can be delivered in smarter economic ways. Thus the challenge is to add value. One way in which we could perhaps do this is by taking a wider view on things. For instance, when a person needs to plan a business trip and the required meeting times and details are known, that person needs to conduct a trial-and-error exercise using airline booking engines in order to determine which flight (based on departure time) will arrive in time to allow for the commute to the hotel or meeting while considering typical traffic delays along the way. The conventional thinking is that one selects a departure date, and will select a return date and the rest is of no interest to the airline. Consequently, much more value can be added if one pauses and considers that this is all derived demand.

Technology and consumer devices such as tablets are spurring new thinking, and a flurry of useful "Apps" (applications) have been made available. But technology has also led to increased price transparency and price shopping. This has made air transportation look more like a commodity. There are ways to address this.

From a pure marketing perspective, the trend from value-based marketing to customer-centric (or "personalization") marketing has merit in that it allows the unbundling of the conventional air transport service into pay-per-use components combined with value-added amenities that passengers are willing to pay for. This so-called retail enablement is a clear need in today's market. But conformist approaches tend to be abundant in an industry where carriers mimic or copy each other's services in order to protect market share, often perceived as one of the overriding goals.

With the amount of duplication that exists in the airline business, it is likely that we will continue to witness a significant amount of continued capital destruction. It is for this reason that *Cruising to Profits* offers a contribution to the ongoing debate on techniques that will facilitate enhanced, and more importantly, sustained predictability in airline industry profitability. The following section will provide a number of clear observations that describe the issues that plague and undermine airline profitability. Subsequent chapters will propose alternative management approaches to restoring the core of commercial success in our industry.

The completion of this book coincides with the industry's 100th anniversary, a significant milestone as well an excellent opportunity to celebrate its successes and assess what conditions could promote further innovation and prosperous results. As an industry that clearly evokes emotion, it has demonstrated volatile upswings and downturns, which to some extent are related to how commercial aviation is managed, if we look, e.g., at its core business model. I argue that while air transportation is about flight operations, commercial aviation is not about air transportation. As such, in this book we attempt to instill an approach that requires a departure from the tubular to a more strategic vision for the industry. I also provide a business transformation methodology as a guiding framework for executing on this vision. It is a compilation of almost two decades of experience, reflection, study and practical applications.

Chapter 2
Statements Setting the Scene

Health Check, Commercial Aviation: 2014

The past decade has been a bumpy ride at best for the airline industry. Security issues, high fuel prices, and the need to cut overhead have left legacy carriers struggling.[ii] The constant quest for additional (operational) efficiency translates in the need for aircraft that enable lower mission costs, although there are clear needs to address organizational inefficiencies of which the economic waste is one of the less evident. By 2020, some people indicate there will be a clear divide between those airlines that operate ultra-efficient fleets and those that will struggle to compete in an era of constantly high oil prices.[iii]

In contrast, one sector has experienced spectacular growth—the Low-Cost Carriers. The achievements of the low-cost sector are enormous. In some markets (mainly on short-haul networks), some low-cost carriers have taken the majority share of traffic. The increased competition in the airline marketplace has pushed Low-Cost Carriers forward to test new models, including forming alliances, operating long-haul, and offering more products and services.

For all the economic challenges thrown their way, the airlines are trading fairly in recent times. Airlines are reasonably more focused on applying some restraint in flooding the market with additional aircraft and service frequency (to produce more sellable seats and cargo space), which provides some temporary relief on yield. The easing in some of the other conditions has also helped, such as the cost of oil, and thus jet aviation fuel[iv]. While the industry overall was expected to produce a USD 12.9 billion profit in 2013[v] and USD 19.7 billion in 2014[vi], economic growth (which historically is the driver of financial performance) remains slow. Recovery is protracted and cyclical, and anticipated profits can be instantly wiped out by a single economic shock or natural disaster. Or even a sentiment.

But even if there is some temporary relief, familiar concerns over high fuel costs and other crises like those seen in the Eurozone continue to cloud the horizon[vii]. By the same token, the key issue is whether the approach to rapid incremental capacity deployment continues, as we started to observe in mid-2013. On the other hand, there is growing confidence that airlines realize there is a need for them to be transforming their business.

Historical Commercial Performance

In the aftermath of September 11, 2001, the airline industry collectively lost more money than it had made in its entire history combined since inception. It lost almost USD 12 billion in 2001 and over USD 225 billion in 2008 during the mortgage-related financial crisis[viii]. Even today, some carriers are losing millions of dollars each day while they continue to carry on as a "going concern," pending the outcome of cost-reduction programs that are part of turnaround plans that maintain the same business model but expect different results.

"Sustaining the unsustainable is no longer an option"
– Chris Tarry, Principal, CTAIRA

Key Facts Lying Beneath the Surface

Before I address and propose management and governance frameworks for improved airline management, it is important to outline the observations and thinking that drive us to conclude that, fundamentally, commercial aviation requires a reset at a level that is commercially viable in order to reassert its role in global trade.

I base my observations on my experience in management facilitation and business consulting work, as well as on customer analysis, and I issue them by taking brief 360-degree views at some the practices in airline management. The observations underline the need for a rethinking of current business models and for promoting further evolution and innovation.

I distinguish between two levels of structural concerns (and in some cases of clear flaws) underpinning the observations. Overall, commercial aviation suffers from industry-level for-profit conflicts that have been plaguing the business ever since it was deregulated in the USA (1973) and increasingly in international markets. At a company-level, the airline-business models utilized are affected by numerous anomalies that impede a transformation to commercial sustainability and paving the way for success. A number of essential factors are at the heart of the structural quandaries or predicaments of the airline industry. Let me explain.

Airline Industry Woes: Industry Level

First, more people travel by air than is commercially viable for the airline industry itself. Also, while it is true that our industry does generate indirect benefits for other industries (e.g. tourism, trade, humanitarian efforts), it itself does not commercially gain from these indirect or derived benefits, even though it is a business and not a social service. Furthermore, the industry has not been able to rid itself of the nationalistic connection that people and governments attach to commercial aviation, in that traditional flag carriers are considered of importance for national security and need to be maintained at all cost, further fuelling a persistent overcapacity in world air transport markets.

The unrelenting inefficiencies that continue to exist in the airline industry are exorbitant and unsustainable, especially given the now ever-present economic or other market-related shocks or pressures. There are simply too many aircraft, too many seats and cargo space offered, to generate a sufficiently profitable return, one that needs to cover the cost of capital and to allow contributions toward future innovation and investments.

The airline industry is not rightsized. Also, the fact that many national carriers each focus on anchor or key economic hubs and hub-and-spoke systems feeding long(er)-haul flights is inherently inefficient and leads to a great amount of service duplication around the world. Most capitals or large cities receive service from national carriers that all feed and accumulate traffic (pax, cargo) by tapping into other carriers' home markets that vice-versa have similar practices and offer flights to the same destinations through their own hubs. Compounding the overcapacity dilemma is the fact that competition for market share in civil aviation centers around frequency of service, so that in short-haul markets we often see hourly flights between a given city-pair, while in international markets one can easily expect daily or twice-daily service. Given this traditional nature of the business, around 18-20 percent of all capacity (seats) or up to 40-50 percent of cargo space suffers from spoilage (it flies unoccupied).

In essence, the frequency of service and the "scale benefits" are blatantly overestimated. However, given the strong focus on competitiveness for the air transport commodity, airlines are reluctant to take the risk to rightsize the network and the service levels to match the profitable market segments they can capture. Top-level numbers (revenue / turnover / traffic volumes) and market share are still perceived as key drivers of profitability, but should be perceived more, in all honesty, as really secondary to such emotional or status-driven goals as those related to which airline or airline grouping is the biggest and has the largest fleet in the world. Even more, all this takes place while the direct correlation between size and profitability is non-existent. There is, however, a masked correlation between size and market share and for reasons other than better service or a loyal customer base. I refer to them as "economies of market dominance."

Secondly, another structural issue is the following. People that travel by air (or cargo that is transported by air) do not consume air transportation as if it were the product they ultimately sought to acquire and enjoy, as they do with consumer goods. The demand for air transportation is a purely derived demand, in that travel is a means to another end. While this may appear to be an obvious statement, it is a fundamental characteristic of the airline industry that is often overlooked. One has only to look at airline advertising or to observe the relentless focus by airline marketers on services and amenities that ultimately do not serve any other purpose than making traveling appear somewhat more enjoyable. With the exception of premium economy-type services, which offer somewhat of a more differentiated product, the end product offered by most airlines is a commodity.

The impact that the derived nature of air-transport demand has on price perception and willingness to pay remains one of the deep-seated challenges to aligning fares with total costs. Arguably it is so because airlines are seemingly reluctant or incapable of educating the public on the cost of air travel. Also, they are unsuccessful in outlining the benefits derived from air transport in comparison to other benefits that can be enjoyed from the expenditure of the same monetary value. On this issue, airlines often mistakenly assume that they are competing with other carriers and their fares for the same passengers. Referring instead to the simple case of a family with an annual discretionary budget needing possibly to decide between building a swimming pool in their backyard or a vacation on another continent demonstrates how easily "competition" is misunderstood. The cost of air travel and fares needs to be reframed against more effective price positioning frameworks. This way, better associations can be communicated, associations that are in agreement with applied pricing psychology. According to the latter, outlays or sacrifices match perceived benefits. I will discuss this in further detail later in this book.

Given that the airline industry, and its growth, has so fundamentally altered the shape of the world, and more specifically how people and goods are brought to market, it is remarkable that these benefits are not reflected in airlines' financial results. For one, airlines connect people so they can conduct their meetings and trade. Also, airlines lift shipments and cargo, allowing exporters to work with importers around the globe. All this is achieved with a full throughput time of no more than a few days (from any airport to any airport), thus feeding global supply chains that allow products to reach shelves on other continents and in other nations without the public realizing how they were sourced.

Full-fare business class and rush shipments or special transport sent as air cargo aside, the plain fact is that while airlines facilitate global trade, they do not enjoy significant parts of the benefits of such economic exchanges. This can indeed be considered a fundamental quandary of the industry.

A third structural jam is of geo-political nature. From a political standpoint, the stringent regulation that exists regarding, e.g., the bilateral agreements, the Freedoms of the Air between nations, the controls on slots at airports, as well as curfews, has made the airline industry one of the most regulated industries in the world. It inhibits entrepreneurship.

Fourthly, while the hub-and-spoke system was instrumental in allowing airline growth and increasing the feasibility of service international/intercontinental markets with larger wide-body aircraft, the same system is inherently operationally and commercially inefficient during economic shocks. Also, this same system has permitted many airlines to grow beyond their natural size, further fuelling industry capacity, bringing down industry load and utilization factors, thus spurring undifferentiated price competition.

Arguably, the hub-and-spoke system may face a global decline, driven by higher kerosene prices and the fact that modern existing aircraft as well as those that are proposed will have the ability to connect any two cities worldwide with lower density aircraft that are capable of flying ultra-long-haul sectors. This will also impact on the Middle-East carriers that have capitalized on the use of Sixth-Freedom traffic to build their hubs in Dubai, Abu-Dhabi, and Doha, much like previous generations of airlines with small home markets did (in particular KLM, the now-defunct Sabena, and former Swissair).

Also, the obsession with service frequency that moved from the domestic domain and is now replicated in international markets, in no small part due to alliances, is only contributing to the industry's woes regarding operational inefficiency (waves of activities requires peaks in resourcing/staffing) excess capacity, again leading to ongoing price battles.

Interestingly, some airlines have gradually increased hub-and-spoke routes in favor of those to the hubs of their immunized joint venture partners. This is what Delta Airlines has done recently in an effort to increase unit revenues and improve profitability of its transatlantic operation. As a result, some of the "spoke cities" have lost service or witnessed a reduction in it. Essentially, providing too many feeder services from spokes into main hubs at low utilization and low revenue/yield levels is untenable and in modern (economic) days should be discouraged, unless airlines gain from a wider economic benefit.

In markets where surface modes can provide an attractive alternative as a substitute and where "over-hubbing" has caused economic turmoil, a restructuring of the regional airline model is needed as well. In order to illustrate, about 82 percent of European scheduled contract flying is currently delivered by low-profit-making in-house subsidiaries. Notably, during the 1990s, when regional airlines operated as feeders into major full-service carriers' networks, we saw the proliferation of the ACMI[ix] model. However, the ACMI model shifted all entrepreneurial responsibility to the major and caused complacency at the regional. Today, it will be required to rationalize the feeder model and to separate them as separate businesses that require their own business model.

It appears that the "contract flying" or franchise model will be a more successful model going forward, not in the least because of the avoidance of union issues around the use of other ACMI-based contracts. In addition, new aircraft technology will help restructure the regional jet operation, as for regional jets[x] trip costs are much more important than seat-mile costs, which are weighted heavily in the single-aisle narrowbody markets.

Nonetheless, industry-stress mitigation techniques will always involve cost cutting and often service reductions. This is the core of the ongoing conflict between network planners, marketers, and commercial airlines managers dealing with pricing and ancillary revenues.

"Cost cutting is a continuous way of [airline] life; we need to work on it all the time"
— Temel Kotil, CEO Turkish Airlines.

Airline Woes: Business / Company Level

The previous section described a number of industry-level dilemmas that the airline business needs to address in order to rectify its lingering profitability issues, and that requires true leadership from captains of industry in collaboration with pan-governmental bodies. It is a matter of strong leadership, not of management, as there is a clear distinction between the two. Although we are no advocates of stronger regulation, industry discipline (relative to capacity and pricing) could arguably only be brought about through some form of "lite" regulation protecting the industry from itself, its shareholders and the public by reducing ongoing capital destruction. Alternatively, markets should be completely open because no half-solution is more optimal.

First, I often argue that most people within the industry take a narrow, "tubular" view of the airline business, meaning that as part of marketing efforts to position a service product the central focus tends to be on the tube or aircraft and on what happens inside during flights. By behaving this way, the airline marketers and even strategists lose sight of the fact that the demand for air transport is a derived demand. As such, the underlying demand that is driving or making people to travel is not sufficiently considered as part of a more analytical exercise to better align services to that demand. This narrow view of the airline business leads to framed, constricted discussions on what can be considered for renewal or innovation, because only a subset of the full picture is considered. Too many assumptions are made and predetermine the scope of what people believe they can change or control. Consequently, the business never really fundamentally changes, and what all airlines end up doing is copying or imitating in-flight products and matching fares.

Thus, to break out of the framed scope and view of the business — i.e. the assumed identity and role of aviation in the world — becomes really important.

Secondly, while airlines trumpet personalization and attempt to recognize individuals using the frequent-flyer programs, by default the very nature of air transport and related services is mass delivery. There is only so much personalization that can take place in flight, and passenger processing at airports can fully undermine any attempts for personalization. Priority boarding and a symbolic curtain between cabins are hardly substantial tools in personalizing service; also, the timing of service on board is driven not in the least by passengers, especially in economy class.

Also, so many people interact with travelers that the likelihood of one staff member impacting on the travelers experience negatively is very high. The very fact is that throughout the various touchpoints and potential interactions with customers, it is impossible to create personal relationships and offer personalized service. There are too many constraints, including regulatory ones such as security screening, customs / immigration, and the very fact of riding in the same aircraft at the same time. However, if one takes the focus off the air transport part of the traveling experience and again considers the driving force of the demand for air transport, better insights could easily lead to more personalized approaches to service offerings around and starting with the need for travel, rather than the travel itself. This more holistic approach would in turn require a much more sophisticated approach to segmentation. It would also dictate an intelligent integration between the data that is collected through frequent-flyer programs, general marketing and business intelligence.

A third business-level issue is that service differentiation attempts still do not drive lasting price premiums. Even though airlines collectively invest billions world-wide in the refurbishment of aircraft interiors and new business-class beds, seats and the latest in-flight entertainment technology (IFE), this can mainly be interpreted to be necessary in order to remain relevant and competitive in the business, as it does not really enable the airlines to ask for lasting price premiums for these services. Most loyalty in the airlines business is artificial and driven by loyalty programs, not loyalty to the services. A separate section of this book focuses on this element later on.

In addition, product distribution is at the heart of commoditization. While air tickets were one of the first and most successful products to be sold on the Internet, this very same distribution channel has caused a fundamental shift in purchasing power toward consumers. At the same time, comparative shopping tools have clearly indicated that the number one factor in purchasing air travel is price, regardless of attempts by airlines to differentiate their products or services, most recently through increased retailing or merchandising. In many cases, the subtle differentiation efforts airline managers focus on go unnoticed by the traveling public, or are not a deciding factor in terms of willingness to pay. What is worse, product and service differentiation could not be communicated through the traditional distribution channels (such as the GDSs) or even during the early days of the Internet, and as such selling tickets via the Web only encouraged further price comparison shopping and commoditization. Despite efforts to create branded-fare products with different attributes, airlines have never fully recovered from this Internet-driven commoditization. Also, the inability of GDSs to display enhancements of the product offering properly is a real barrier to innovation and to the industry's ability to generate a return on its investment.[xi]

In recent years, there have been attempts to address the distribution and product/service visibility in the various distribution systems (selling or reservation systems), as vendors realize they did not cater well to the needs of, particularly, airlines. IATA has launched an initiative around a proposal to create associated technical standards, so that airlines do not go off in different directions (as it happened in the decade-long struggle to achieve interoperability on the e-ticket). IATA Resolution 787 presents this idea and lays the foundation of what is referred to as "New Distribution Capability (NDC)." Unfortunately, the resolution was written in abstractions and its vagueness led many to have their own perceptions and pre-conceived notions. Essentially, 787 is about engendering a new way for airlines to sell products and services designed to appeal to particular (and individual) tastes and preferences, on the back of customer profiling. That is to say, the customer would have to voluntarily share personal information so that personal offers can be creatively created. Some in the trade (particularly travel agents and the global distribution systems—GDSs—used by these agents) argue that Resolution 787 is in essence a vehicle to arrive at discriminatory practices with clear violations of data and personal privacy. However, it is time that the airline industry took charge of its offering (with or without intermediaries) and used new (merchandising) techniques and platforms as vehicles to connect better with the end customer. In these approaches, customers would be presented with the opportunity to identify themselves (if they chose to do so) and the system would provide them with more and better information on which to make decisions. In the end, the traveler would decide what personal information would be shared, but the more would be shared, the more the customer would benefit in personalized services. This is about the customer, not about protecting travel agents (who would nonetheless be able to book these products on behalf of those customers that prefer to use a travel agency regardless).

Airlines have not yet been fully able to capitalize on the opportunities that online distribution presents, particularly mobile (smartphones and tablets). In particular, they have not been able to address the core problem of commoditization. This is mainly related to the fact that airlines are pushing for the sale of airline tickets or air transportation, without investigating further what drives this demand and how it can be incorporated in other bundled services in a more persuasive manner. We need to remove the base assumption.

Further, economies of scale and scope are always referred to as a driving force behind the popular hub-and-spoke system and behind the alliance and other collaborative marketing arrangements. However, evidence suggests mergers (i.e., increased scale or consolidation) and alliances are effectively attempts to capitalize on "economies of market dominance" than efficiencies. In fact, with such conflict between bilateral and multilateral alliance grouping interests, the alliance strategy in many cases has lost focus and attractiveness. It has also resulted in a confusing web of competing interests that impede the distillation of true benefits to an individual airline, especially in those cases where the relationship between carriers is collaborative in some markets (O&Ds and through traffic) but competitive in others (O&Ds that do not fall within the scope of the alliance or collaborative arrangement). It has as such become a cost and revenue accounting puzzle that can be misrepresented from many different angles.

In general, alliances do generate benefits and allow an economical market entry. However, there is also a significant cost to entering these arrangements from both an operational (lack of flexibility, commitments and passenger services liabilities) as well as from a purely commercial point of view (less commercial control and loss of market response flexibility).[xii] Cultural issues are also another permanent area of conflict, even in the most tightly arranged deals.

Then there is the upswing and popularity of "low-cost" operations, which we argue is now dated. Everybody wants to be low(er)-cost, but the money is made in crafting a differentiated product that is perceivably different, unique, and sustainably so. Low-cost carriers served a purpose for some time—of breaking down old-fashioned conventional airline pricing structures—and were able to stimulate traffic by moving people out of trains and cars and into planes in short-haul markets. But the low-cost skies became overly crowded and saturation forced a natural correction in commercial aviation markets. The low-cost carrier (LCC) model, which capitalized on the high-cost and operating complexity of full-service airlines and challenged the status quo so successfully in the early 1990s, is "tired"—it itself is running out of steam.

The low-cost segment is making tactical moves in their network and fleet as they struggle for position and prepare for the next expansion wave, potentially even in foreign countries' home markets[xiii]. However, demand has saturated, and even low-cost carriers need to innovate differently, often leading to discussions on becoming a "hybrid" carrier, which would only increase their unit cost. There are limitations to growth, and mergers between LCCs have not always proven to be efficient, while the integration costs have in some cases made them approximate the cost of legacy business models. When competing head-to-head, LCCs clearly also fail to differentiate. With so many "Low-Cost Carriers" now facing the next phase in their business model life cycle, many of them see no alternative than to mold the model. Their purpose in doing this is to mimic the more conventional full-service carrier business model by targeting business travelers, especially corporate, by participating in all—including the more expensive—distribution channels, and by offering premium services in the form of a separate "premium" cabin. The fundamental issue with the "evolution" of these carriers into more conventional models is that they are coming out of a growth cycle in a saturated segment only to aggravate industry capacity and utilization problems.

"In the future, you will compete with everyone. We have to learn to compete with everyone.[xiv]"
– Bjørn Kjos, Chief Executive, Norwegian

Prices and fare product design logic are lopsided. As long as air fares are not related to the cost of providing the service, but placed on an artificial framework attempting to align perceived value with willingness to pay (and depending on existing competition in non-stop or direct/connection markets), new business models should and will challenge this approach, as it is inherently not customer-focused or customer-friendly. In most industries, product pricing or prices for services are relatively straightforward, but the late 1990s and early 2000s have seen the influence of pricing psychology and pricing techniques create havoc and confusion in many people's minds. Particularly the technique of unbundling products into features and core and optional services, to create à-la-carte personalized products and to upsell (upgrade to premium levels) or cross-sell (offer items related to complementary products and services), all aimed at enticing or inducing incremental spend, has been tremendously popular.

But the airline industry has been particularly keen on creating fare levels and fare products that are based on forced market segmentation. The use of the word *forced* is to reflect the punitive nature of segmentation applied by airlines. Fare products were created and "fences" were erected in order to separate for example price-sensitive leisure travelers from the less price-elastic business travelers, particularly those traveling on corporate expense accounts. Thus, the characteristics of short-haul vs long-haul travelers on either leisure or business trips were used to create products with fare and usability restrictions that would ensure that business travelers could not make use of discount fares offered to leisure travelers, even when booking early. In recent years this was relaxed somewhat, mainly due to the market pressure of successful low-cost carriers that challenged the conventional model in order to stimulate traffic and make their mark in marketing and promotional campaigns.

Nonetheless, the recent approach of branded fare products is essentially a renewed attempt at a comeback of the conventional fare products from the 70s-80s, albeit in a slightly more modern fashion. The only difference from the old scheme is that only one fare type ("bucket") would be open at the time, whereas today the fares are presented online in a matrix, so that the service features and amenities can be compared. If one selects a deeply discounted fare, the "punitive" nature of these fares is that there are no or little frequent flyer miles, no status miles, and no ability to change the flight/date/itinerary (short of a hefty fee and applicable fare changes).

At one end of the scale, travelers are penalized for not willing to spend more on their air travel. At the other end of the scale, full-fare offers full flexibility and all the perks. In other words, today's pricing is based on the principle that discounts are only available based on sacrifices, and that premiums ensure rewards. From a pricing psychology standpoint, this is an appropriate and effective technique, yet the issue in the airline industry is that these sacrifices and rewards are poorly communicated and accepted by the general traveling public for historical reasons (i.e., at a given time these services were typically included in the base fare). One of the causes of this situation is that airlines typically relied on travel agents to handle their bookings; another, that airlines have never fully embraced the reality that pricing and marketing cannot be separated in an Internet-based economy. Airlines' internal departments cannot work in silos, as they are still mostly organized today. Positioning, communication, and marketing campaigns around a priced product offering are now very tricky, in a very open, public environment with a very vocal broadcast audience. I tackle the issue of silos and governance in our proposed **"BeProFit"** (BPF) framework further down this book.

The bottom line is that the traveling public is acutely aware that fares are not related to the operating cost or to the full cost of providing the service. People think in terms of distance traveled and related costs, and are quick to point out that short-haul point-to-point flights cannot be more expensive than connecting flights overseas. Adding to the difficulty, this issue has never really been addressed properly, which only fuels the adversity between airlines and their customers. To change compass, some airlines are contemplating to begin operating on a "pay for what you weigh" scheme[xv], essentially applying an excess-baggage type pricing model, so that individuals that weigh more than a set average weight will have to pay an additional fee, to counter incremental costs related to fuel burned (or possibly the additional seat they may require). While this approach seems "fair," it is not so in light of the inconsistencies that exist in airline pricing today (and hence it may be premature).

Also, airlines realize they cannot publicly come out and say that they take advantage of the lack of competition in some markets to see how much the market will bear before it becomes suboptimal in terms of matching supply to demand (utilization and load factors). The point that is being made is that for a service industry, there is little focus on true customer service and customer satisfaction, clearly undermining true loyalty.

By the same token, Revenue Management (RM) has failed to drive lasting incremental benefits. Also, it is flawed in situations that present changes to the underlying business model. In recent years, its innovation has not kept up sufficiently with changing business models and revenue management practices are now surprisingly sub-optimal. RM is a blind horse when not adjusted for more accurate business assumptions, particularly as it is still treated as a back-office analyst-driven function that does not encapsulate the overall commercial engagement with passengers and cargo customers.

The challenge for RM analysts is to eliminate the bias inherent in the mathematics underlying the business-as-usual mix optimization models that have been used over 30 years. One of the more blatant flaws is that RM was based on the assumption that demand exceeded supply and that fares and booking curves could be manipulated upwards toward departure, but this assumption is invalid when applied in a generic way. Also, for instance, revenue management processes and software packages were developed against the backdrop of a fare structure that involved a forced segmentation based on whether somebody was an early-booker leisure traveler or a late-booker business traveler that needed more flexibility in terms of cancellation, say the ability to return in the same business day or during the workweek. Discounted fares were only available on a return basis or with a Saturday night stay requirement, clearly imposing an artificial "segmentation" onto the market and thus the perceived value of certain fare products. Recent advances (or "software patches") have allowed the management of branded products/fares that are available simultaneously, thus to some extent value-based pricing is somewhat better coordinated with capacity controls today. However, the approach is far from holistic and is not driven by customer-facing activities.

Fundamentally, since RM cannot articulate its logic to the traveling public, it will continue to be challenged, not in the least by new entrants who argue that there are more customer-friendly ways to connect and align with the willingness to pay of the clientele. The punitive nature of RM, as with ancillary revenues, will pre-empt and continue to deter sustainable business models.

Another area of business-level conflict is the field of loyalty and customer relationship management (CRM). In essence, frequent-flyer programs are punitive in nature and the structure of FFPs undermines true loyalty. We have often argued that FFPs today are structured so as to create loyalty to the loyalty program, not to the carrier and its services. Redemption is challenging, and premium flights are accessible only by burning a disproportionate amount of accumulated points. FFPs are also used as a mechanism for guerilla marketing tactics in order to squash new entrants or competitor service enhancements essentially making the bonus points the only differentiator. FFPs have little to do with true loyalty management or customer-experience management as they do in other industries, but they are nonetheless somewhat effective in that a captive audience (shared with other carriers and the programs they are also a member of) will behave in certain ways in order to qualify for next year's status, to name just one example. However, the underlying hindrance is that "loyal" travelers are not necessarily the most profitable travelers, and carriers are still wrestling with this predicament.

This book presents a management and governance model that will facilitate a transformation in this area as well. Also, I contend that in order to fully realize the potential of loyalty management using allied business technology, airlines must be innovative by taking the customer relationship management outside the current comfort zone. CRM and loyalty management can pave the way toward integrated marketing and attain the overall goal of joint customer revenue and loyalty optimisation, by implementing interfaces to other key marketing systems, such as those found in revenue management. The current generation of CRM and loyalty systems falls short of supporting these goals, due to a limited scope and focus that does no longer reflect today's travel industry, as well as owing to obsolete technology platforms and high costs. Next-generation solutions that are unique in their ability to permit innovative interfaces and allow a cohesive overall marketing system will be the key enabler for organisations trying to create competitive advantage.

Moreover, ancillary revenue tactics essentially mask a troubling industry. In many industries, ancillary revenues came to life as complementary value-added services or features that the public appreciated as beneficiary. In the aviation sector though, generally, ancillary is often seen as a weapon to neutralize the ups and downs of the fuel price.[xvi] The airline industry embraced ancillary revenues as a technique to decompose service items or amenities that had previously been part of a bundled service product, in order to charge incremental fees. This can be considered a punitive approach to unbundling, as average fares for the basic air travel component did not decline. Examples include fees for checked bags or even carry-on baggage for some low-cost carriers such as Spirit Airlines. Even though there are clear commercial benefits in the ancillary revenue approach, the fact is that air travel has been commoditized to the extent that pressures on fares are prevalent. Charging for some items (e.g., bags) by making them appear optional can mask artificial fare increases and is evidence of an industry with a structural pricing problem.

In addition, behavioral, economic, and technological changes are dictating fundamental transformation. A forever-changing customer base, the evolution from Generation X to Y to C ("connected") — a clientele that demands personal recognition and wants to exercise personal choice. Software programs have attempted to use analytics and data mining for profiling and for segmentation based on trip purpose, but oftentimes general marketing campaigns include messages to frequent flyers that are ill-suited given what should already be known about them.

Finally, we maintain that current airline governance pre-empts true innovation. Ultimately, the way airline companies are structured is one of the key challenges in overcoming the stalemate regarding innovation. With such a core focus on aircraft rotations, scheduling and pure flight-related operations, as well as with the typical silo-driven functional management of airlines that delineates the on-field/in-flight and off-field office (marketing) environment, it is immensely difficult to encourage true innovation that is beyond the business models we are familiar with today. Conceptually, considering an airline industry that focuses on facilitating trade and communication beyond the core aspect of flight services between airports does not bode well with divisional heads of most airlines I have worked with. Yet, one of the key opportunities for the airline industry is precisely that, i.e., moving into the periphery of the air transport business-model boundaries we are familiar with today. This book was written in order to table such opportunities and present them in an executable manner.

While airlines are trading fairly in early 2014 and have more focused on manageable growth since 2009, recovery remains protracted and cyclical and is disproportionally subject to economic shocks and natural disasters. There is growing confidence that airlines realize there is a need to fundamentally transform their business.

We distinguish between two levels of structural concerns that underpin key observations. First, commercial aviation suffers from industry-level business conflicts that have been plaguing the industry since deregulation. One key aspect is that we find that more people travel by air than is commercially viable in today's commercial model. Also, it is evident that the industry generates indirect economic benefits through the economic multiplier effect. These are benefits from which the industry itself does not gain commercially.

Second, at a company-level, anomalies in airline business models impede transformation to commercial sustainability, often due to the "tubular" view of the business and the lack of true differentiation. Consequently, we developed and present a strategic management-and-business-transformation methodology around the recognition that commercial aviation is (1) about communication, in its wider sense, and (2) about well-being, in its personal significance.

CRUISING TO PROFITS
Transformational Strategies for Sustained Airline Profitability

Chapter 3
Restoring the Core

As described in the previous chapter, a number of key observations are made to underscore that after one hundred years of existence, commercial aviation is not sustainable as a profitable industry in its current shape and form and/or with conventional business models. Before we look at ways in which the core can be restored, it is, however, interesting to briefly reflect on how we got there, and on what some of the more fundamental factors were in commoditizing the business.

In the early days of commercial aviation, travelling by air was a privilege that was only within reach of the affluent and wealthy groups of the population. Flying was glamorous and attracted a great deal of attention, while often inspiring people that did not have the means to travel by air. The industry was heavily regulated, and so were air fares, allowing airlines to pass on operating costs with a sustainable profit margin, due to the willingness to pay that existed for this mode of transport. Due to the high degree of regulation, coupled with relatively small aircraft, airlines were able to enjoy sufficiently high passenger load factors at healthy margins.

Initially, the notion of various cabin classes as a means to segment the market according to customer needs and willingness to pay did not exist. In a way, one could arguably describe the service levels at what would today be classified as "business class" in a single-class configuration.

With the arrival of the jet engines in commercial aviation, during the late 50s, and with a wide adoption of first generation aircraft with turbine engines, such as the Boeing 707, also came a new reality. Not only did jet aircraft significantly extend the possibility of non-stop missions over sector lengths that allowed considerable time savings, the larger size of these craft required in turn the carrying of larger fuel loads, which also resulted in larger fuselages, permitting a larger number of seats for revenue passengers. To some extent, this was the first step toward making air travel more accessible to other market segments, with less disposable income.

However, the real turning point in civil aviation can be traced back to the onset of the Boeing 747. Initially designed for the U.S. defense industry with the purpose of allowing the transportation of large troops, the aircraft was to be the largest aircraft ever made with the capacity to carry up to 400 passengers or 90 tons of cargo. While the aircraft was to be and did become the "Queen of the Skies," it almost bankrupted the Boeing Company at the time, as up to 50 orders were cancelled by the U.S. government due to a more stabilized international political environment.

What saved the Boeing 747 project, as well as the Boeing Company, was industry pioneer Pan American Airways (Pan Am), for long the largest international carrier and the first to offer around-the-world flights. The sheer size of the aircraft astonished many and attracted many spectators at airports frequented by the plane. However, the seating capacity represented an almost 100 percent increase relative to existing aircraft, such as the Boeing 707, and represented a challenge to commercial departments in regards to achieving high utilization of this perishable inventory. The aircraft did represent significant operating economies due to the dense capacity and as such the lower costs per available seat mile were passed on to new market segments such as leisure travelers and VFR traffic[xvii].

The Boeing 747 classic aircraft allowed the creation of multiple cabin classes designed to separate market segments and associated service levels. Subsequent derivatives such as the Boeing 747-300 included a stretched upper deck, which propelled a number of airlines to introduce lounges and even piano bars in order to further instill a distinct recognition of those that purchased First of Business Class air travel[xviii].

Notwithstanding these early innovations of airline marketing, business realities struck when increased competition and overall industry capacity reached such levels that it became increasingly important to generate incremental revenues. As such, precious real estate, which was initially granted as public roaming space, quickly vanished, in order to make room for additional revenue seats. By the same token, service levels in economy class gradually eroded, with the addition of rows and the resulting deterioration in leg room.

Besides advances in aircraft technology, the trend to deregulate the airline industry further opened the door for some of the realities we are facing today. Deregulation initially started in the USA in the domestic market, where rules were relaxed on intra- and inter-state travel, start-ups, and fares. It was essentially the backbone of the success of Morris Air / Southwest Airlines and many airlines ever since.

While clearly advantageous to the general public in offering more choice, high frequency of service and lower fares, deregulation did have a profound impact on an industry that was nonetheless fairly immobile, due to strong labor relations and entrenched unions. The trend to deregulate commercial aviation spread from domestic (USA) markets to international markets during the late 1980s and 1990s, especially when marketing collaboration and alliances became popular as a means to circumvent restrictions on market access, traffic rights, and foreign ownership in airlines. Notably the alliance between Northwest Airlines and KLM at the time was an industry-leading collaboration that ultimately evolved into a true joint venture across the Atlantic. But alliances have had dual and in some cases conflicting results, which I will describe in more detail later in this book.

CRUISING TO PROFITS

Transformational Strategies for Sustained Airline Profitability

Essentially, deregulation facilitated a more opportunistic and entrepreneurial way of conducting business as airlines, but also led to the basic premise based upon which airlines started to compete for market share, which is service frequency. Further, the hub-and-spoke network system that became so popular in the early 1990s allowed airlines to combine traffic rights (Freedoms of the Air, particularly combining fourth and fifth Freedoms) in order to bring people from third countries to their country, to then transit them onto other (long-haul) aircraft destined for other third countries. Airlines were able to take advantage of the lower cost per seat mile (economies of density) of larger long-haul aircraft but required the feed from other source markets (origins) in order to make this viable. While this makes economic sense — given that the cost of Jet Aviation A-1 fuel is low enough to incorporate some of the inefficiencies inherent in combining short-haul with long-haul, it has led to an exponential growth in airlines networks including of those carriers that had a particularly small home market (e.g., Switzerland, the Netherlands, Belgium, Finland, Singapore, Hong Kong prior to the hand over to PRC rule). This growth was fundamentally in excess of true demand and has led to overcapacity in world aviation markets.

CRUISING TO PROFITS
Transformational Strategies for Sustained Airline Profitability

Today, the bottom line is that the capacity situation continues to be a plague in the business. Airlines compete for market dominance, but often cite "economies of scale" as a driving force for mergers and acquisitions, even though extensive analyses and research could not identify any significant evidence for true economies of scale. Coupled with a somewhat marked loss in direction about the role of commercial aviation, a rethink is useful.

While in other industries or businesses most retailers focus on a wider view of how customers engage with them and their brands, the airline business is still very much transactional. But e-commerce and mobile technology are causing customers to leave digital trails and with appropriate retail enablement there is value in building customer profiles in real time, based on historic transactions and customer-choice based modeling.[xix]

A holistic approach to and view of air transport are necessary in order to address the fundamental profitability issues facing the business. The lack of this view as well as a lack of balanced production and sub-optimal or ineffective and inefficient organizations is preventing the business-model components to add value to the product offering synergistically. As such, it is worthwhile to look at a commercial optimization and governance model that may help to rectify these challenges and should surely spur further debate on the topic.

But the ultimate underlying shortcoming in airline design is missing the fact that aviation is not purely about transportation, but about **(1) communication** (people traveling for business and relationship needs) and **(2) well-being**, i.e. people traveling for personal needs. In both these areas there is significant competition for the same (discretionary) dollars from outside of the direct air-service operating field. Only by looking beyond the framework of airport and aircraft operations may we find opportunities to reposition the role aviation plays in a more holistic view.

BPF — The BeProFit Business Transformation Methodology

Drawing on business and management experience as well as other professional expertise and academic contributions, we have developed a business transformation management methodology that encompasses a business model reassessment tool and many related toolkits that allow executive airline management to elevate applied strategic management to an industry level, which enables them to remove obstacles and facilitate the creation and operation of a sustainably profitable business. The approach is getting endorsements and some case studies will be provided as part of the *Cruising to Profits* program.

There are three pillars to restoring the core of sustained profitability, each with their own methodologies. Figure 1 on page 89 provides a pictographic overview of the overall model and its building blocks. The three fundamental pillars are:

1) Redefining the role of aviation and improved segmentation/targeting

2) Rightsizing the industry (balanced supply and demand)

3) Transformational strategies
(including the governance of effective transformation)

The transformational strategies should be as developed under our **BeProFit** (BPF) framework, which focuses on a fully aligned business model with supporting, separately identified but aligned business functions, underpinned by their processes, into a single business-transformation-management framework. The latter is unique and does away with traditional management techniques or organizations found within airlines.

Redefining the role of aviation

It is important to make the world understand the importance of aviation. As mentioned previously, we categorize the essential role of aviation as two-fold, i.e., in facilitating (1) communication and (2) promoting well-being. While these may appear to be more philosophical or conceptual classifications, they do underline the essential roles that aviation fulfills, and they hold, once explained and applied to day-to-day management.

In more practical terms, aviation enables people to connect and conduct business, which in turn makes it possible for exporters to ship goods that are imported in other nations and contribute to other local economies. With aviation and mobility being global, the airline business plays a vastly important role in facilitating economic trade and humanitarian aid across the globe.

CRUISING TO PROFITS

Transformational Strategies for Sustained Airline Profitability

Even though commercial aviation represents a USD 711 billion industry in terms of revenue, its external benefits are a significant multitude of this in terms of its overall reach and impact. IATA, among many other associations and organizations in the field, has as one of its goals to identify the benefits that aviation generates for consumers, public finances, and the global economy, even though it is difficult to agree on a single numerical value. But, as said, there are other — non-economic — factors that describe the benefits of aviation, such as the ability for people to connect, mingle, exchange, or simply visit family. These include psychological benefits.

In terms of pure economic growth, it is often said that:

Aviation **benefits** passengers and freight with swift, cost-effective transportation;
Aviation **contributes** to the overall economic growth of nations;
Aviation **provides** significant revenues to national public finances;
Aviation **creates** large numbers of high-value jobs;
Aviation **delivers** extensive catalytic benefits to international trade and tourism.

Where the debate can be widened is in that while the airline industry creates various external benefits, it does not typically actively participate in or profit from the natural extension of pure air transportation. Also, even though airlines are cognizant of the fact that people travel for a wide variety of reasons, their marketers are typically mainly preoccupied with a more aggregate level of segmentation around the high-level purpose of travel (classified as either "business," "personal or VFR"). Many more micro-level segments can be identified to allow airlines to get closer to one of the current trends in marketing, that of personalization.

Marketing in commercial aviation could become more sophisticated if the overall trip were placed in full perspective around the overall driving force and the personal needs associated with the purpose of the trip. Let us consider a person traveling for the purpose of attending a conference. That person would have several needs and wants pertaining to the trip and would likely need planning tools around:

Which date and time to arrive (not which date to depart)?

What hotel options fit the (corporate) budget if planned independently?

What commute and transportation options to consider for getting to the hotel, or elsewhere?

How long the commute is (if traveling the same day)?

Which people are likely to attend that the person could possibly network with for business purposes?

Which entertainment or sightseeing options exist for the duration of the trip?

Which people may be traveling on the same itinerary that it could be interesting to commute with?

Which people may be interested in joint activities?

Which communication tools are available to stay connected throughout the entire trip and stay?

How the overall stay can be enhanced with any needs that may come? And the list can go on.

In most cases, airlines do not know enough about the people they carry to be able to draw a full picture of their possible needs and desires. People are mainly or only categorized based on the type of fare they purchase and are often labeled as "business" or "leisure," which in the past tended to be sufficient in terms of how fare structures functioned.

Yet in today's world, a much deeper understanding is required in order to get closer to each individual and put the trip in overall perspective. When this is done, it allows the identification of many more requirements and wishes that people have and as such allows airlines to propose value-added services and amenities that fit each individual's needs in a much more sophisticated fashion.

The ultimate goal is for airlines to offer a bundle of services that encapsulate and cater to the needs and wants of each person in a much more holistic manner by taking care of the person far beyond the traditional "booking-to-deplaning" cycle. In fact, there is an opportunity to offer a personalized service if one considers airlines as facilitators in communication and well-being. Airlines could consider an array of possibilities in widening their view of their roles, by:

Creating intimate partnerships with tourism organizations;

Aligning with conference associations;

Getting involved in event planning;

Venturing in consumer/finance product markets;

Facilitating human networks and meeting platforms around specific themes;

Allowing human connections prior to trips to continue throughout the trip and after the return;

Providing communications networks prior to and throughout the journey.

With regard to cargo, similarly, a widening role of airlines in and an ownership of the larger supply chain would necessitate airlines to consider the derived nature of air cargo demand and the constant shifting dynamics in supply chains across all commodities. By involving themselves with other entities and players active in these supply chains, airlines should be able to identify opportunities to add value (e.g., new products and services) and/or carve themselves out a role that would cushion the individual shocks that can be felt if one is only on the "air" receiving end. However, a separate management book will be dedicated to cargo as part of the *Cruising to Profits* series.

Nonetheless, it is imperative for the airline business to look beyond the airport-to-airport transportation role and focus on integrating its service offerings in a wider travel-related consumer trail that can span from sophisticated trip planning to full merchandising with regards to all of the travel- and experience-related components. Providing full support in event planning, the hosting of events or meetings, platforms to find and negotiate meeting space and/or organize all trip and communications-related items can essentially allow airlines to provide turnkey solutions for a great experience. The technology that exists today, combined with a trend of various booking platforms and technologies converging, is an area that should be explored in more detail, in order to better connect with the traveling public.

Some suggest that internalizing social media tools and tactics would be an opportune way for obtaining more input and ideas on what the requirements, needs and wants of the traveling public are. One would have assumed that with the practices of general marketing, CRM, and more recently the full-blown FFPs airlines would have a good handle on such information, but it is surprisingly unstructured and not well-organized or shared. To some extent one can also view the social media and sharing themselves as being partially the result of poor customer service and relationship management. But now that social media enable a very public way of voicing complaints, airlines are keen to respond and rectify issues much more quickly, due to the exposure. This did not exist in the past.

Conversely, social media can be a useful tool to browse through content, comments, and suggestions, and to connect differently with individual people and travelers. The industry can make use of this to its advantage and feed ideas to the internal product and service development experts so as to respond constructively to consumer needs and wants.

Rightsizing the Industry

It is very important that we recognize that the profitable market demand is much smaller than some want the industry's scale to be, and that there is no value — other than a negative one — in stimulating a finite demand.

We mentioned earlier in this book that the industry is too big to be commercially viable, in the sense that it is a business that has been structurally plagued by overcapacity. Traditionally, low-load factors were less of a concern, as average fares were higher and aviation was profitable. However, in today's competitive environment, it is important to increase the density in discounted service classes (basic economy class) in order to maximize incremental revenues for each flight. As well, higher load factors have been paramount in meeting break-even levels or in achieving a minimum level of profits.

Nevertheless, the rapid expansion of new entrants and the aggressive capacity deployment of others, notably in the Middle East and Gulf region, have given rise to shifting air-traveler traffic patterns or transit flows and, more importantly, to an excess of capacity, given the world's air transportation needs.

There exists also a saturation point in terms of stimulating traffic, but that does not deter ambitious carriers that are predominantly interested in attaining a certain size and market share at the expense of overall industry commercial health. Thus, while some carriers deploy capacity-discipline tactics, others bring down industry load factors and create further pressure on fares and yield, because they would like to see as many planes as possible carrying their name on the fuselage. Unfortunately, some of the fundamental challenges boil down to that ego level.

But collectively the captains of industry could focus more on those segments in air-transport demand that are profitable and could limit the subsidization of other segments. Of course, this would require a commitment to abandon the pure "size argument" for more commercial pragmatism. As in any other industry, we do not have to carry each person, and the general public has to recognize there is a cost to providing the service.

The above then also requires another rational look at the tangled web of alliances. Today, alliances count for 60 percent[xx] of the global passenger traffic, and the various alliance groups are making all efforts to close the loop or "blind spots" in geographical areas that are not yet connected within the alliance network. In any event, the alliance movement has now reached a point at which the addition of new member airlines will slow down.

Besides, there have been many benefits of these tie-ups and commercial arrangements, but at the same time with the ever-growing membership within airline alliance group the issue of "coopetition" has become a real and complex issue. For instance, Delta signed an agreement with Virgin Atlantic for a 49 percent stake in the latter and was aiming to form a transatlantic partnership that would be separate from Delta's existing transatlantic joint venture with SkyTeam partners Air France-KLM and Alitalia. While the three carriers would coordinate transatlantic flows, there is a high likelihood for possible conflict, and it is increasingly difficult to separate the business interests of all concerned. Another example is that of Star Alliance, where Austrian Airlines has been very vocal about the issue that the joining of Turkish Airlines has resulted in a more competitive environment between them, despite the alliance arrangement, because Turkish Airlines' focus is to fend off Middle-East based carriers in short-haul (source) markets. Airlines even admit to this complex abnormality.

"[...] that of course all members remain competitors, despite cooperating in many fields"
— Mark Schwab, CEO, Star Alliance Services

Increasingly, the benefits of alliances are intangible and somewhat politicized, because of the fact that the interests among the various alliance members are not truly aligned and the participants continue to act as opportunistic individual entities. In some cases new members in an alliance group are arch rivals of other existing members and specific origin-destination by origin-destination agreements have to be reached, which then become very difficult to administer and account for. Alternatively, long-lasting arrangements that have been in place for over 10 years can come to an abrupt end through the association with another carrier, for instance, by means of a merger. To illustrate this, US Airways' membership in STAR Alliance will be discontinued and replaced by participation in oneworld because of the merger with American Airlines.[xxi]

Today, the stakes and risks are higher with regard to forming or joining alliances than they were when alliances first started to appear, in the late 1980s, and when they proliferated, during the 1990s. The popularity of alliances as market-entry tactics and seat-share instruments has signalled a shifting landscape in that participation in mature markets (such as North America and Europe) is no longer sufficient in global commercial aviation and that covering the blind spots in the Middle-East and Latin-America is crucial for a successful network. This has also made alliance entry a much more consequential decision that requires thorough due diligence.

The above is especially true since alliances can be very expensive, as witnessed during the process of Aerolineas Argentinas joining SkyTeam. Also, the cost of disconnecting TAM from Star, following the merger with LAN and the "under-one-roof" strategy that alliances maintain regarding airport terminal operations, is very high. In addition, a growing scale of alliances and alliance groups adds more incremental complexity the more members such groups contain. Also, the decision-making starts to decelerate more, the more carriers participate. But they are still often seen as the single best technique and instrument to provide access to source and "hinterland" markets that otherwise would not propel an airline network's growth or would not contribute to its traffic density. A question just remains, in that one has to wonder how much duplication in services we need, and how many alternative traffic flows the world needs. Some therefore wonder how this alliance and capacity structure would work out should the oil, and thus aviation fuel, become cost-prohibitive, something that, on the other side, might pave the way for a natural cleansing and restructuring of the industry.

Alternatively, the increasing environmental attention the airline industry is getting from a carbon-footprint perspective will be a challenging force to cope with, given the abundance of overcapacity, the duplication of efforts, and the crowded and inefficient airport and navigation operations.

While redefining the role of aviation and rightsizing the industry as more macro-level industry leadership topics, the next chapter focuses on what airline leaders can do at a business or company-level from a transformational perspective. It provides a framework consisting of three toolsets that will facilitate a fundamental change process toward sustainable profitability.

Despite a recent cushion, traces of the long-term trend toward commercial depression in commercial aviation go back to the principles of deregulation and to the premise of airline network competition coupled with the entering of wide-body long-haul aircraft on the market deployed in hub-and-spoke networks. While economies of density, scope, and scale are often touted, the real remnant commercial value is more accurately related to stronger market presence, an aspect that drives alliance group growth and mergers and acquisitions. Restoring the core in commercial aviation requires the recognition that air transportation is a derived demand and needs to be approached outside the current framed scaffold that somewhat holds commercial managers hostage. Three key components to restoring the core of sustained profitability are (1) a redefining of the role of aviation at macroeconomic and microeconomic levels; (2) an industry-driven rightsizing of the industry by balancing supply and demand in concert with its role; and, (3) a framework of transformational business and organizational strategies.

I propose this framework as an ensemble containing a Business Model, a Process and a Functional Integration methodology and designate it as "**BeProFit**". The framework comprises a number of toolkits. The next chapter introduces the framework, and a number of applications will be presented and described throughout the remainder of this book.

Chapter 4
Transformational Organization

The third pillar in the **BeProFit** business-transformation-management methodology is precisely the transformational organization, and itself consists of a number of methodical steps. Before this is described in more detail, I introduce the overall framework in a pictographic way below, as it helps in navigating through the tool.

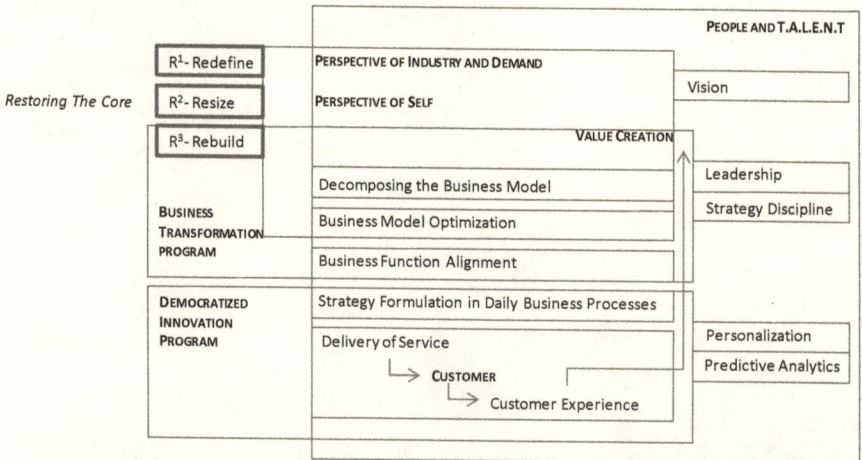

Figure 1. Cruising to Profits Business Model Optimization & Business Transformation Methodology

A high-level description of the components of the framework is as follows:

True business transformation starts with redefining the role of commercial aviation and with restructuring it to a more natural size and scale. This requires an industry-level vision and involves personalities with strong leadership skills that can remove obstacles. I discuss transformational leadership and the human capital multiplier in detail in the next book, Volume 3.

Rebuilding a sustainable commercial aviation business requires a business transformation and democratized innovation program. The proposed business transformation program consists of tools to break down the business model into core functions that need to be aligned with the role airlines play in the industry and in global trade (business model optimization). Once the business model is fully decomposed, the departments (functions) that make up the airline organization can be restructured for streamlined governance so that each function/department, job, task and customer touchpoint creates the desired customer experience as part of the core business model. Since frontline employees are most exposed to and interact with customers, the experiences and observations that are gained by such employees need to be captured and fed into the work of those responsible for formulating strategy. The democratized innovation program is a method for involving the end customer in the strategy formulation and the design of the service delivery. It is a trend that will continue, spurred in part by social media, but one that requires careful management.

Democratizing innovation also means that this innovation will help airlines create services and service products that can be personalized to the individual. It also requires predictive analytics based on past and current customer behavior and choices.

Ultimately, the added-value creation is done jointly between the airline and its customers and will produce unique services and, more importantly, ways for reaching the customers and engaging them on a continuous basis in their daily lives. Somehow, the lives of airlines and their customers become intertwined because there is daily interaction between the two. A relationship has been constructed that has little to do with air transportation, but more with how one is connected to their business and social world.

While the overall framework can be replicated, the people that make up an organization — not products — will truly make the difference with regard to the creativity, the end product, and the profitability that are generated. In my human capital multiplier methodology, I demonstrate that leadership is about the removal of obstacles and that people generate the profitability once the business model is applied in line with the role of commercial aviation and once the governance model empowers people to act accordingly.

Organizing for Effectiveness

In Volume 3 of this book, I elaborate on how people, their talents and organization's culture can be aligned to ensure employee fulfillment and company profitability. This section will not dwell on this topic any longer than highlighting that self-motivated and focused people are crucial to the adoption of effective management frameworks such as the one proposed further in this book. I demonstrate that people impact on profitability directly.

One of the most common complaints made by airline managers is that while senior management talks about "strategy" and improving the commercial performance of the company, every individual has their own interpretation of what the company strategy is. In many cases, they are high-level buzzwords and vague steps toward achieving the overall goal. This is, in part, due to the fact that actual strategic moves are usually only known at the board and the top executive management level, in order to ensure that other people in the company do not leak key information to the market. As such, long-term plans are typically formulated and explained in such a way that they could easily apply to any other peer enterprise in the business. What is worse, in most organizations "strategic" plans are merely budgetary plans prepared predominantly by finance.

This aside, and despite many years of academic, professional and consultants' work involving success stories of management models, or proposing frameworks that are made to fit past success stories and attempts to isolate contributing factors, it is still very difficult today to find a working method that looks at an overall business model and attempts to get a handle of all components in a holistic but also manageable and cohesive manner. I argue that it is fundamentally because business models need to be decomposed before they can be rebuilt.

One of the core problems is that while many can describe an airline's business model and describe its components, such a model does not provide us with a framework or toolbox that can act as a concrete guideline for day-to-day management. It tends to paint a picture that can be communicated, but not executed.

What I find is that it is crucially important to make the translation from the business model to the functional level in order to provide leadership on how the various functions are to come together as a whole and execute toward common goals from within. Essentially, the business functions exist to deliver on each goal and to do so in a synergistically coordinated fashion, so that the leadership team can steer the business model and long-term corporate future successfully.

For instance, we can often give the blueprint of a low-cost airline and describe the components of its business model. But it does not mean it is clear for an airline management's team how to carry out its commercial and operating plan against this blueprint and how to organize for success in terms of organizational delivery, especially across the business functions and supporting business processes. This explains in part why airlines with similar business models, operating in similar markets at similar cost levels, can have varying degrees of effectiveness and profitability.

In the airline business, we often attribute lack of profitability to external factors, such as costs, inflexibility regarding organized labor, and especially capital costs and the cost of Jet A-1 aviation fuel. But like any business, the airline business needs to mature and deal with input costs (and the variability in or fluctuation of related prices) simply like a *cost of doing business*. Consider this analogy: a restaurant does not need to adjust prices or apply surcharges because the price of tomatoes is higher due to a bad harvesting season or other issues in the supply chain. A restaurant patron would not realistically care. Similarly, passengers should not care about the input costs of airlines unless by exposing it they have some influence on changing it (they do not). By the same token, if one makes a restaurant dinner reservation today for a dinner next week versus a few days later, the price of the menu does not change.

In some cases, things work in theory but not in practice, but the airline business has also defied many by demonstrating that some things do not work in theory but they do in practice. An example is where full-service carriers compete in some of their (OD) markets but have alliances in others, and have arrangements with other carriers with whom they have a marketing agreement in the first, but compete in the other. This has often been dubbed "coopetition" (competition + cooperation). But the general idea is that this is still sub-optimal and simply a temporary technique to circumvent restrictive bilateral agreements between nations. In a normal fully competitive world, these practices would not be observed.

Consequently, we need to take another look at airline business models and contribute to the ongoing work in this field by decomposing airline design and proposing an approach to restoring the core and use a business model optimization toolkit that I summarize to be compatible with the "Business Model, Process and Functional Integration" methodology (**BeProFit**). It combines three techniques into a single coordinated framework that has a unique angle to it when used properly.

BeProFit focuses on the alignment of commercial airline functions and commercial processes by viewing the entire service product, delivery and experience through the eyes of the consumer. It requires us to structure the airline company in such a way that we initiate the planning process with the purpose of the (1) communication and (2) well-being needs that the each individual in the customer base has. There is no proper term for what we explore, but it is a reference to a constructive contribution to the ongoing debates on true transformation in the airline business, under the guiding principle that we redefine the role of aviation and bring capacity in line with true needs.

While this needs to be done at an industry level, it is recognized that this is very difficult in a highly competitive business. As such, it requires true visionary leadership beyond the airline boards, in a collaborative fashion. We cannot fully tackle that issue in this work, and therefore we start at the carrier level, and subsequent series of this publication will explore the next steps up.

What I have done is apply a business sense to it by putting the customer at the forefront of business model (re)design. This is a radical departure from conventional airline planning around network planning based on an assumed or observed (historical) demand.

There are three key approaches we explore and propose to deal with the "theory vs. practice" gridlock. If commercial aviation is about connecting communities in the world to facilitate communication and well-being, then we should structure the company in such a way that it fully supports the objectives our traveling public is trying to meet. This is very different from attempting to make the flight itself as pleasant as possible using the latest of in-flight amenities and services.

The approach I have taken is a phased sequence and involves four key activities and steps:

Business model optimization. This consists of finding the equilibrium of competing elements and components in the business model, competing for the same resources or having conflicting objectives. For any individual airline, this involves the decomposition of the business model into building blocks from which all business discrepancies can be removed. It also allows executive management to formulate how their airline's business model carves out a unique role for the airline given the role the industry has in a wider perspective. That is, an airline is more than a myriad of destinations connected by flights.

Overlaying of business model components on business functions. A reverse process then validates how business functions support the desired business model in the existing governance structure.

Example: While people talk about a company's "value proposition", which departments in a company drive this value proposition, and how do the various departments' pulls come together to achieve a proper delivery of this value proposition?

Example: How does an airline's marketing, frequent-flyer program, e-Commerce, pricing, revenue management, and sales departments integrate their functions so as to deliver on the key component that is driving the business model to be successful?

Where do these functions appear on the business model blueprint in an integrated or harmonized fashion?

Aligning business functions. This is achieved by focusing on their interrelationships, with the purpose of supporting the components of a harmonized holistic business model.

Example: Airline sales is typically concerned with incremental sales of seats through corporate deals, while general marketing is more concerned with supporting general sales. Conflict arises between CRM and Frequent Flyer

Program (FFP) departments vis-à-vis general marketing, because oftentimes the interests of CRM do not align with those of general sales or marketing. The issue is exacerbated by Pricing and Revenue Management, which tends to control the capacity allocation to tariff buckets including redemption seats on purely once-off transactional basis. This is just one illustration of how the business functions do not work in tandem, while exposing an area with inconsistent service delivery mechanisms as experienced by the customer.

Embedding value creation-based strategy formulation in day-to-day processes. The true exposure airline staff has to customer experience and expectations is face-to-face and through the various communication means, especially social media. We argue that potential strategy identification happens every day at different levels of the organization but are not captured in any informal or formal way. This is a renovation of the value (profitability) chain and its role in creating or identifying tactical and strategic opportunities by allowing it to feed corporate processes with the purpose of creating a workflow that delivers on customer and shareholder expectations. It boils down to capturing ideas from the floor and using those that have merit in longer-term planning, given the various business functions can come together to bring it to full fruition (as per the previous steps). We will elaborate on this in more detail in sections that follow.

Example: How does day-to-day sales and online activity drive new product design by feeding into the strategy formulation of what products and services to sell in order to solidify the value proposition of the airline?

One of the most challenging aspects of my approach is that it has significant and fundamental implications on how we look at the use of human capital, the required skill sets and the process of strategy formulation compared to the people that currently hold positions in airline management, marketing and sales.

More importantly, our approach shifts the role of strategy formulation at tactical and business strategy levels down the organization to those that are closer to the day-to-day operations and have a better pulse on the market from an operational perspective. This is then used in longer-term corporate strategy formulation. Thus, I depart from the notion that strategic planning is an isolated "top-level" process that is remote from daily activities and is conducted in closed-room war room sessions once a year. Strategy formulation can be daily; at least to the extent that intelligence should be captured and fed into the "strategy bank."

Following my tested approach, I will provide examples of how we have done this in practice, followed by a section illustrating the implications on business requirements.

First, it is important to articulate what is understood by business model so that we can decompose it for redesign and reconstruction so that is better aligned with value generation, or simply said profitability drivers. There are various ways in which business model components can be described and many classifications essentially differ only in the terminology used, not in fundamental principles. But a common and recent categorization is to describe a business model by:

Value proposition
Customer segments
Customers / customer relationships
Channels
Revenue streams
Key activities
Key resources
Key partners
Cost structure

The above sequence is not a typical sequence as proposed in academic literature but what I have done is apply a business sense to it by putting the customer at the forefront of business model (re)design. This is a radical departure from more conventional airline planning.

While some of work in this field provides input and clarification on the business model components, the individual headings can create confusion and no two people will infer the same meaning from their names. For instance, for some, "value proposition" could mean a unique differentiating feature or competitive price. Communicating this for a company across all levels is even more difficult, but necessary.

In order to clarify further what each business model component consists of, the section below provides more details.

Value Proposition

The air transportation service as perceived as a means to a personal or business end for a specific customer market with a unique bundle of benefits for which the customer is willing to pay $x. At a high and overly generalized level, it equates into the price/quality/utility for a targeted customer group. It includes the touchpoints through which the customer interacts with the brand/company, how the delivery of the service/product as well as the payment is effectuated, and what the perceived productivity levels are from a customer's perspective.

Customer Segments

These are the identifying groups or subgroups of the customer base that share sufficient similarities in terms of needs, wants, and preferences, so that they can be targeted with a carefully designed product as a group. In the airline business, we tend to distinguish between business travelers, leisure travelers or vacationers, and VFR traffic (Visiting Friends and Relatives), but this is overly generic and many more layers of detailed segments lie underneath.

Customers & Customer Relationships

Customers and customer relationships are the clients of the company that purchase and use the airlines' transportation and related services, and deal with all customer service staff that interact with, deal with, or otherwise act as customer touchpoints throughout the overall cycle. Departments that are involved in this also include the ground staff, customer relationship management (CRM or frequent flyer program) staff. It can involve different groups of people depending on whether the touchpoint is direct (airport), online (web support), or offline-by-phone (reservation desk).

Channels

The channels are the distribution and entry points through which customers reach the airline, which include the telephone, the Internet, third-party websites (such as OTAs — online travel agents) and mobile devices.

Revenue Streams

Airline revenues have historically been driven by the sales of tickets for air travel and the carriage of cargo and mail. In recent years, airlines have focused on generating additional revenue by acting as merchants for hotels, car rental agencies and other travel-related businesses, but also by unbundling the travel experience into individual components that become optional for purchase. Examples are extra luggage allowance and in-flight food or entertainment for purchase.

Key Activities

The key activities in the airline business revolve around the core activities involved in air transportation, thus aircraft and flight operations and all enabling functions such as dispatch, crewing and maintenance.

Key Resources

The key activities necessary to keep and airline afloat are evidently finance, fixed assets such as aircraft, as well as people.

Key Partners

Airlines have had business partners in working with airports, but on a more direct level and especially since the late 1980s, key partners in the airline business would refer to marketing and joint-venture relationships between carriers from different countries and geographical nations, often generically referred to as alliances, although the word alliance typically should refer to deeper and more integrated business relationships and structures. From a marketing standpoint, key partners are often the merchandising partners involved in the product offering around the Frequent Flyer Program (such as department stores).

Cost Structure

The cost structure of an airline is the input but also end result of what goes in the value proposition in order for it to be offered to the public.

Airline business models can often be described and articulated, but it is more difficult to introduce a transformational program into a business that has a framed view of its own business-model life cycle. In this chapter, I introduce the **BeProFit** methodology that supports strategic planning and business transformation for sustained airline profitability.

I argue that leadership is about the removal of obstacles and enabling change. Management is about assigning resources and completing tasks. The **BeProFit** framework offers a translation from business model vision to synergistic functional level coordination across all departments. It requires all functions to support and deliver on the same goals through each business model component. The application puts the customer at the forefront of business model redesign as well as service delivery. This has ramifications throughout the airline organization.

Recognizing that many functions (departments) have conflicting interests, our approach is a phased sequence of key activities, i.e., (1) business model optimization, (2) alignment of business model components with functional departments, (3) alignment of business functions themselves, and (4) creation of value-based strategies in the daily business processes throughout the organization.

The transformational organization recognizes that all existing business functions contribute to the composition of the value proposition to the end customer and as such need to be in full concert. This is a departure from the current function-based organizations we find.

Chapter 5
Business Model Optimization

BPF Methodology, Step 1: Business Model Optimization (BMO)

Management pursues optimization of the business model in order to maintain a competitive edge and remain relevant in the global marketplace. For airlines, this is a steep task, as there is little differentiation between carriers and many services find strong substitutes. In addition, most behavior, products, and amenities can be copied in this business, making constant refurbishing investments the sole method of staying ahead, and a very costly one. Yet, with limited aircraft manufacturers as well as limited In-Flight Entertainment (IFE) and seat suppliers, one cannot speak of true differentiation. Such a differentiation has to be derived from taking a more holistic view of the role of aviation, combined with the technology-enabled service delivery component, also with simply the tactical advantage of the ability to service certain markets at desirable frequency/density levels.

However, this again is more directed at market share than strict profitability.

I find that the level of BMO needs to be elevated to consider other aspects around the periphery of the typical air transportation model. As argued earlier, I find that airlines are challenged to define their role in the airline and/or larger industry and struggle to articulate their purpose. This makes it difficult for them to work through a true BMO exercise, as there are few unique aspects around their business model that can be tweaked for value-added competitive positioning. It would be necessary to move away from the traditional transactional model and focus on personalized offerings through retail enablement and a deepening of relationships that can be constantly renewed through open innovation. Open innovation refers to a process in which the customer is an active participant in the generation of ideas and the creation of new products and services. It is sometimes also referred to as the "democratization" of innovation.

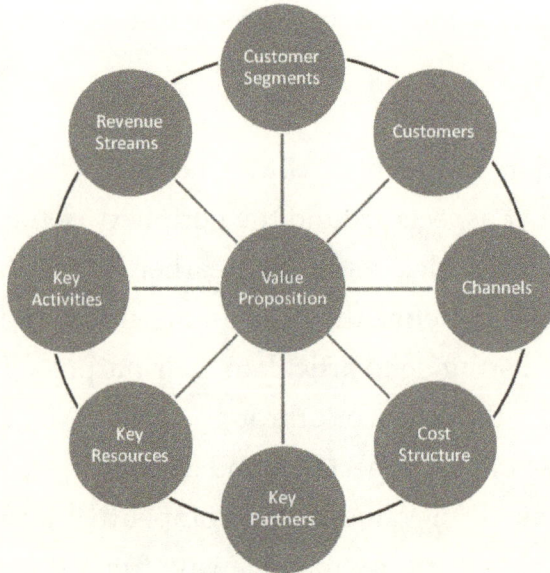

Figure 2. Standard Business Model Components

It is a tremendous effort and task to align all business model components in such a way that actions can be formulated from them. The overall value proposition is the summary of the business model blueprint as all business model components need to act in concert.

The real challenge in exposing business model components is that one quickly realizes that airline departments are active in or impact on many of the levers.

Further, each business model component requires a full alignment with another component and thus has a *"strategic touchpoint"* in that blueprint. For example, if key partners (P) are essential in a model, than we need to consider the cost (C) of delivering key activities (KA) through the right channel (CH) to reach the right (C) in a specific customer segment (CS), before we can conclude it represents the right value (V) to be a proposition. My point is essentially that they are all interrelated and that therefore a business model blueprint in itself is highly complex from a *delivery* integrity and consistency perspective.

The delivery aspect is also emphasized. This is because, while all of the business model components may in itself represent clear and tangible value creators, they must all come together perfectly for the customer of the service product to be satisfied while "consuming" the service throughout the entire consumption cycle and at any single touchpoint at which the service provider may intervene or be present. This needs to work in concert before the company can attain its goals—its mission—and be profitable sustainably. Simply said, even if an airline does a great amount of planning and offers a differentiated product by offering a special—in-flight and overall—experience using the best of its aircraft serving tactical markets where it can perhaps avoid stiff competition, if its staff ruin the experience for the travelers at any of the points throughout the trip, this will have a lasting impression on the part of the customer and will undermine all of its efforts. This is particularly the case when working with other airlines under alliance arrangements. Airlines have little or no control over how service is delivered on the "at arm's length" end.

Taking a different approach, if ease of use and overall service is considered to be of first priority then an effort can be made to view the world from a customer's point of view that the starting point is really the purpose of the trip, for which the actual air transport may be a necessary "bad." But in order to attend to the traveler's needs (e.g., she is going to a specialized conference but has other logistics interests and needs and cultural interest), we may need to reverse-engineer the way travel is booked. For instance, if one needs to attend a meeting overseas and knows the starting time, oftentimes one is forced to run several trial-and-error origin-destination service options by departure time in order to find arrival times. That is because traditionally the airline industry is focused on the fact that people <u>want</u> to travel, and thus pick their departure day/time and then the return. The value proposition for these conference people would be very different. How a service product like commercial aviation is "consumed" actually starts at the entry point of each channel (telephone, mobile/App, internet search engines). The customer also needs to provide input on which service aspects and items are of interest and add value to the experience. This is essentially about relevancy.

We thus focus on the interrelationships of the components and argue that it is in this area where "business model optimization" can occur. That is to say, rather than isolating and managing each component — as is typically done — we shape our thinking using an underlying assumption treating the overall business as a single function that needs to be commercially consistent and well-aligned like a well-oiled mechanical machine. This is difficult when it involves people to carry out the alignment and coordination, and is as such not an automation opportunity because the process does not yet integrate people and technology sufficiently or to its maximum potential.

Business Model Optimization Applied

As mentioned earlier, there are many ways in describing business models or in displaying the various components of what makes up a business from a generic point of view. What is important though is to define revenues/profit and customers as an end result toward all efforts are aligned and focused. That requires a clear commitment on the type of customer that is envisioned and targeted. Only once those customers and/or customer segments have been clearly defined can airlines and other companies clearly lay out how these customers will be identified, serviced, and supported, throughout not only the booking and travel cycle, but ultimately throughout their life cycle. That means that all activities, resources, partnerships, the channels through which these relationships are maintained, and the cost of all of these combined needs to be fully coordinated and focused around the customer and customer segments that have been defined and targeted. An analysis of all costs will guide the airline in its decision-making as to whether the revenue and margin that can be generated from each customer justifies the company's efforts and associated costs.

What I am essentially saying is that each customer of the airline should contribute to the its margin generation, because I feel that by continuing to focus on wider customer segments and maintaining a practice of cross-subsidization among the customer segments served, airlines will continue to lack focus on where their value proposition meets market demand *and* the market's willingness and ability to pay.

Should there be customer segments that cannot be served profitably purely from the airline's perspective, then airlines should share in the commercial benefits that are derived from a person's travel and communication beyond the air transportation portion.

Alternatively, should other entities in the hospitality, leisure and entertainment business require people in their respective customer segments to travel at a price that is not compelling to airlines, then they should feel free to negotiate overall bundles that do.

In this chapter I argue that the scope of business model optimization needs to be widened to consider other aspects around the periphery of the typical air transportation model. At the heart of a successful commercial aviation business is the value proposition offered and moreover executed and delivered to its customer base according to customers' personal expectations. This requires us to better align the departments in an airline (the business functions) with its overall business model, an alignment which is the topic of the next chapter.

I focus on the interrelationships of the business model components that can deliver on the departmental alignment and argue that it is in this area where "business model optimization" can occur. That is to say, rather than isolating and managing each component—as is typically done—I shape my thinking using an underlying assumption treating the overall business as a single function that needs to be commercially consistent and well-aligned like a well-oiled experience management process. The engagements I led have shown that, using my detailed toolkits, business model optimization is the first constructive activity in creating unique value as a company.

Chapter 6
Business Functions in Business Model Optimization (BMO)

BPF Methodology, Step 2: Aligning a Component-Based Business Model with Business Functions

A cut-and-dry mapping of a business does not actually provide any meaningful way in driving anything. It is a static picture (or "skeleton") of a business model that helps depict some key focus items of a company's overall business. More importantly, I argue that airlines are not effectively organized to deliver on a promised value proposition, because there is no clarity on who actually owns the customer, and this lack of ownership can lead to a high level of complacency, especially in highly unionized environments. This will be tackled in later sections of this book.

Only by layering business model components over the business functions of an airline and then carving out new business processes can we convert this into a toolbox that can be executed. Conversely, i.e., reversing the process, this is especially effective when one attempts to draw out how business functions support the business model components, since more than one business function impacts on each or multiple components.

However, to enhance a company's business model, the transformation must cut across the silos of functions, risks, and assets, in order to capture the most significant value drivers in an airline. In other businesses, intellectual property can be a good example of such a value driver. In the air transport business, a value driver can be the access to key airports and convenient departure/arrival slots, but it does not tend to get more strategic than those operational aspects.

How to operate and which processes will be streamlined can be questions included in an airline's business-model-related evaluation that can be broken down into the functional level, as business processes can be designed at that level. But that means that an overall business process will have be designed and drawn across the functions. I provide several such examples in subsequent sections to demonstrate how we have done this.

A level down from BMO is the necessary, and difficult, translation to the actual day-to-day of an airline in that we need to establish in terms of how the (typical) airline business functions support airline business models. It is one thing to describe the airline business model of, say, an all-business class seat airline and describe how that looks like on paper in an intelligently-described way, but when it gets to the business level only clear language and execution of plan toward this business model count. It is at the functional level where the internal organization delivers on the success of the business model, and we found this to be the crux of most profitability leakage in the industry. Even when business models are well-designed and fairly unique, the execution involves departmental heads and people that are oftentimes not working toward common goals.

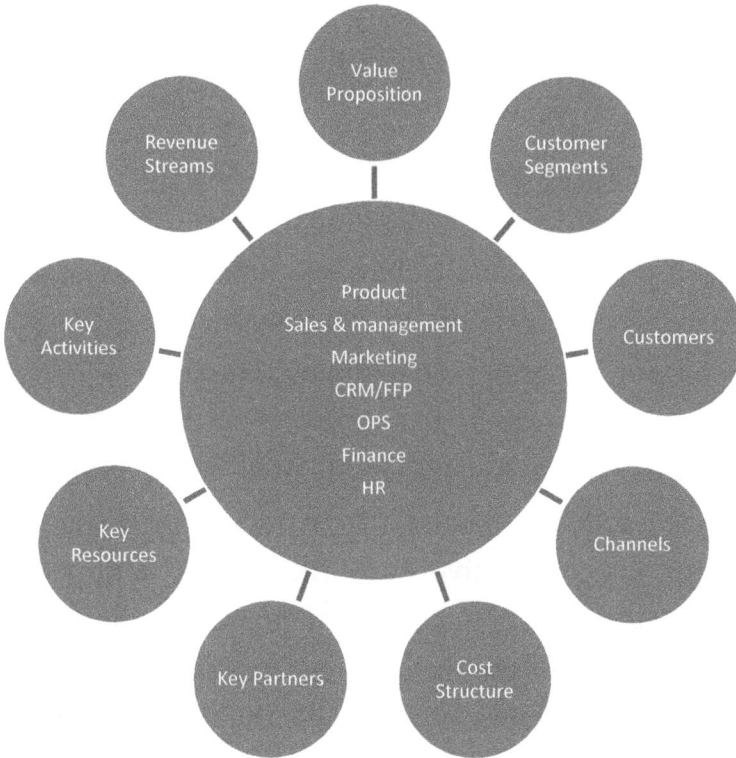

Figure 3. Business Model Components and Business Functions

In the chart above, not only does each business model component depend on and interact with each other, but the various functional departments that run the airline on a day-to-day basis need to constructively work together to deliver on this blueprint. This does not require only focus but also clear leadership.

In fact, most of the airline functions have an influence on not one, but multiple business model components, and it is rare, in my experience, that business functions are organized around the delivery of results toward Business Model Optimization. Consider the following example.

Sales is typically concerned with sale volumes and revenues, product is related to network/flight, and pricing is involved in competitive fare monitoring and ensuring competitiveness, while pure OPS is far remote from the overall purpose of the business as we find it. Even further remote from the business is typically the finance/accounting department.

Airlines juggle multiple customer segments and are generally in the process of manipulating access to the common capacity seats in order to maximize revenues and profits.

One form of business model innovation could be to integrate all components of a business model in a coordinated fashion, rather than viewing them as pure stand-alone building blocks. It is this functionally integrated manner in which the experience is designed and delivered that will be perceived by end customers. Companies can focus on each building block and emulate what others have done, but a smooth delivery through a coordinated business process, in a culture that harnesses an effective and consistent bundle, is difficult to replicate or copy.

In one form or another, each business function in an airline impacts on the "health" of multiple business model components. For instance, a department that manages alliance relationships and joint products will incur costs and impact on margin/revenue contributions (R), as it will impact on key activities (KA), will impact on and require key resources (KR), and will have to deal with the various channels through which alliances (P) and customers (C) interact with the airline. It is very complex to integrate this business function and associated business processes so as to align it to business model optimization in terms of what profitability can be generated from targeted efforts and targeted customers as part of the alliance effort. Determining the cost alone of this single function is a difficult task.

In this chapter I focus on the interrelationships of the business model components that can deliver on the required alignment with departments that make up airlines. It is in this area where "business model optimization" can occur. That is to say, rather than isolating and managing each component — as is typically done — we shape our thinking using an underlying assumption of treating the overall business as a single function that needs to be commercially consistent and well-aligned like a well-oiled experience management process. My client engagements have shown that, using our detailed toolkits, business model optimization and an alignment of departments against the designed business model are the first constructive activities in creating unique value as a company.

Chapter 7
Functional Integration

BPF Methodology, Step 3: Functional Integration (Business Functions)

In most airlines—like in most companies—the various departments that make up an airline are often functioning as silos with departmental heads that have personal attachments to their scope of responsibilities over which they have some level of control. This often means that some people issues can act as obstacles to full and productive coordination with other departments, let alone full alignment or integration.

Also, the same applies from a business functional perspective, in supporting the delivery from an organizational perspective. Typically each business function, take marketing, has its own specific responsibilities and objectives, although they tend to be skewed toward at least one major "anchor" of the business model blueprint. Marketing tends to be closely tied to Key Activities (KA), as the tangible products and softer services are typically found there.

However, inter-disciplinary alignment and integration is crucial if one is to create an organization that fully supports business model optimization and that can take direction from leadership on how to organize and execute changes in line with the overall corporate objectives.

Since all business functions are related, a completely hypothetical and perhaps unpractical idea would be to combine all departments into one organization that is focused around the delivery of all activities under each component toward the delivery of the "value proposition" to the targeted customer. To some extent, though, this could be a disruptive technique to help refocus an entire company's internal organization to deliver the desired result.

It is even more difficult to let departments within an airline perform their functional (i.e., departmental) tasks toward delivering their contribution to each individual "anchor" of the business model and to create at the same time an ongoing workflow that continues to fuel the value chain for future profits and cruise to profits. That is the root of this book. That is, the recognition that business functions must be tied to business model components and that today not many organizations appear to exists for a harmonized effective delivery mechanism of such business models. And so most fail or do not sufficiently innovate.

As stated before, the silo-driven organization and hierarchical governance levels I find in airlines impede innovation and are, most importantly, a significant impediment to optimized commercial performance (maximized profitability).

There is a need to identify the value of each component in the value proposition that is presented to customers, so that measurability is achieved, allowing a steering of the business model, the functional alignment, and commercial optimization from a process alignment perspective (which is discussed in the next section).

An example is event planning. It is possible to track all major events in the world, forecast the traffic they generate, and analyze what logistical requirements these people have. This could be proactively planned and integrated in the outlook or tactical plan of the airline to smooth out peak loads and optimize performance. Longer-term relationships can be forged this way as well.

In order to get to this level of business model management, we need to conduct a mapping of business model components to functional areas that make up an airline. This is the first step to creating deep insights into how we can improve the bottom line of airlines and organize for success (from a governance perspective).

Below, I provide a case and illustration of the diagnostics we made on functional-level integrity.

Value Proposition & Business Functions

Today, airline business models are intrinsically inconsistent, with practices that have opposing results if one attempts to map departmental efforts to the business model anchor of value proposition. A few illustrations or examples include the following:

The overall sales process of an airline is still transaction driven, typified by a clear sense of anonymity of who the customer is, even if that customer is a frequent flyer and logs in using her user name and password. However, at the same time that very customer may be contacted by general marketing as well as the FFP department regarding special promotions, and yet another department crafting other value bundles offering subscription-based programs. None of this is coordinated properly, that is coordinated with the aim of engaging with the customer and designing a more personalized package of service offerings that takes into consideration the person's profitability profile toward the airline.

Even though in theory CRM and RM are areas that should be compatible, in many ways they are currently not. While revenue management is mainly concerned with individual purchase transactions and short-term revenue optimization, based on controlling product availability among customers grouped by broad characteristics, customer relationship management is aimed at attaining overall marketing effectiveness through the recognition of preferences of specific individuals, even though today they are mainly grouped into a few broad categories.

From a value-proposition perspective, and considering our proposed alignment of business functions with business model components, to deliver measurable profitability, the following factors should be considered or be in place:

Open innovation should be embraced in order to expose airline managers directly to the expectations of individual air travel customers so as to reinvent airline's service offering. Leadership should then drive innovative initiatives. Social media can be an instrument in this process and truly facilitate the process by offering a primary research mechanism or even allow one-on-one interaction. This means that marketing and product design essentially work hand-in-hand, if not in an integrated fashion, in order to design and deliver new services and amenities that are in line with market demand expectations. Pricing departments will be closely involved in assessing willingness to pay and in determining price points that stick.

Personalization is a trend that will alter how services are consumed and designed in the future. It requires that all business functions in airlines come together to reassess the impact of personalized service on operational aspects (airport processing and in-flight) as well as on commercial processes (booking and overall experience) with regard to the overall purpose of travel and the air transportation itself.

With an increasing focus on self-service (part driven by airlines, and part driven by consumers' desire to have more personal control over the travel process), as well with the expectation to remain connected to Internet-based applications, there is a multitude of implications on the various business functions that have consumer touchpoints, as well as on support functions such as human resources and finance. For instance, the use of airport kiosks and/or tools that are available online (whether through the Internet or through smart phone and tablet Apps) has an impact on the deployment of staff at airports as well as on the way they are to interact with customers using this technology.

The overall perception of customers and their satisfaction level will depend on the overall experience they have dealing with airlines for the entire scope of their exposure to carriers as related with the purpose of travel. In most cases today that spans from "booking to travel and return travel." However, should airlines get more involved in vacation and event planning, as well as in business communication and facilitation, the commercial exposure to risk — failure or disappointment — is substantially higher if service cannot be delivered as per the promises or expectations that are set.

Experience management from an airline's point of view therefore touches on the entire organization, and consequently on all of the (business) functions that support the service offering and delivery. Failure in one component (for instance inconsistency between online vs offline service offering and customer support) will have an impact on the overall perceptions of the traveler.

As mentioned above, there are abundant benefits in interfacing revenue management to customer relationship management, by deriving important customer-related intelligence and promoting tailor-made products and promotions.

An exchange between RM and CRM business technology would cope with current and future business challenges, such as:

Estimating individual willingness to pay for different products in various situations;

Calculating individual customer value based on the overall repeat business relationship;

Estimating the propensity for upselling and cross-selling;

Estimating the propensity of ancillary revenues (other add-ons);

Unbundling service products and the rebundling of products and features into personalised offers;

Establishing price levels for add-ons based on perceived utility (e.g. what is useful when);

Enhancing analytics, permitting improved market segmentation and targeting at a personal level;

Forecasting the opportunity for redemption traffic;

Dynamically proposing alternative flights or dates, and itineraries based on individual customer value.

New CRM business technology will allow an integration of revenue management intelligence, while proposing new market segments and inventory controls, based both on revenue optimisation and customer life-time value. This will enforce trust and foster an all customer-encompassing appreciation that does away with the case-by-case approach so commonly practiced today. The product unbundling — or differentiation — approach will further facilitate a justification of variable pricing. It would also raise switching barriers for members, as the buyer-seller relationship significantly improves through potential offer personalisation, relevance, and product availability.

The third step in the BPF methodology, which is the inter-disciplinary alignment and integration, is crucial if one is to create an organization that fully supports business model optimization and can take direction from leadership on how to organize and execute changes in line with the overall corporate objectives.

The overall value proposition of an airline can be condensed into a pendulum between perceived sacrifices and rewards. Sacrifices relate to comprises the customer has to make in order to obtain the services required or desired (price, restrictions, validity, penalties and so forth), whereas rewards relate to benefits obtained for those sacrifices (basic service, extras, freebies, upgrades, amenities, convenience, eligibility, FFP points, and so forth). The challenge is that this value proposition, or at least the perception of it, is different for each and every person and personalization therefore represents a significant challenge in meeting the future customer's expectations against the backdrop or constraints faced by airlines. Nonetheless, it is evident that this is no longer within the realm of marketing, but more a required business-function oriented and coordinated effort that cuts across all conventional functions. Airlines struggle to identify with this notion and to make the necessary structural or organizational changes.

Chapter 8
Strategic Value-Creation in the Day-to-Day

BPF Methodology, Step 4: Embedding Value-Creation Strategy Formulation in the Day-to-Day

The final step in the framework revolves around the recognition that in many organizations, including airlines, a great deal of valuable knowledge about customers, markets, competition, and the internal workings and effectiveness of the airline exists but is typically not used to its full potential. In many cases, customer agents or airport staff is treated as operations people and many office support, junior marketing, and commercial staff are perceived as more involved in the execution of strategy and tactics as formulated by senior levels of management. This is inappropriate for two reasons. First, oftentimes it is those staff that experience customers first-hand and obtain a wealth of experience in customer expectations and satisfaction. Also secondly, by viewing people that are not at senior levels of management in the company as people exclusively tasked with the execution of activities as formulated by more abstract levels of planning and management demotivates workers and makes them feel disconnected from office-based functions.

It is our experience that airlines can create sustained and persistent competitive advantage by incorporating the experiences and views and opinions of all staff across the company into both strategic as well as tactical planning. This can be done by capturing feedback, observations, opinions and ideas into a centralized review loop, which evaluates how the business model performs and can be optimized against the external environment—mainly competition—as well as against internal resource constraints.

In addition, as part of a drive toward open innovation and allowing customers to help design future products and services, collaborative innovation can be facilitated and business technology, in particular new software systems, can be made available to make good use of the information, transform, and structure it into intelligence that has true commercial value. Beyond Customer Relationship Management systems, that is.

What is key in todays and future markets is that detecting opportunities and challenges quickly provides distinctive industry positioning and competitive advantage in the marketplace. Being reactive will set airlines behind, as only those that are pro-actively involved in continual strategy redesign will be able to lead profitably. Also, unfortunately, the business model life cycle and product life cycle of new services is getting shorter and shorter.

In addition (and as it relates to ancillary revenues), going forward we need to optimize ancillary charges, rationalize them, and become more professional in everything airlines do. In the case of airlines, we have to orientate ourselves in the aspect of retail, as it is in the high street, and there are many lessons that can be learned from retailing.

What the above implies and entails is that the following functions and systems need to be aligned and ultimately integrated into a business-model-optimization-driven business system:

Pricing;
Reservations;
Loyalty Management (Frequent Flyer Program);
General Marketing (registered customers, database);
Analytics of digital trails on web-based tools (shopping, booking);
Revenue Management (capacity management, forecasting, pricing);
Analytics (purchasing behavior, customer choice modeling);
Customer Relationship Management (customer service);
Financial, Accounting;
Customer Service;
Social Media.

By embedding analytics, intelligence, observations, experiences, and ideas into a feedback loop that is encouraged and rewarded by senior management, it is arguably feasible to have tactical strategy creation, formulation, and adjustment happen every day. Tactical strategies are those small steps that support business strategies and indirectly the mission and vision of a company. They are pragmatic steps in daily activities, like observing what travelers do in lounges while finalizing their plans at destination.

CRUISING TO PROFITS
Transformational Strategies for Sustained Airline Profitability

Strategic planning is not necessarily an annual "planning" exercise driven by financial planning and budgets, but more an ongoing introspection of how the business model performs in day-to-day life, allowing an early detection of changes in the marketplace and/or underlying industry trends. This would be early enough in order to flag issues and enable discussions on future courses of action. The intelligence that can be picked up from day-to-day operations and market exposure has such value that it could set an airline apart in crafting services that span more than airport-to-airport operations and provide a structural differentiating factor. However, one has to listen to and structure information, as well as sift through the data heap to identify what has value.

However, considering the above, the intelligence would have to go through a process of business-function-impact review in order to draw out any idea against the overall "delivery process" of the airline's service, again from looking to booking, to the service experience, and to follow up, however the scope of the service offering. In many cases, it is the overall process of how services are delivered and experienced that spells the difference between success and failure, which is why some airlines succeed or fail even though they offer the same perceived service as advocated by marketing (but not in terms of how they are delivered to the customer).

Therefore, the service delivery aspect of new service attributes has to be assessed against the checklist of how they impact on, and how they should be embedded in the:

Overall product offering

Promotional campaigns

Pricing and presentation of pricing

Various channels or distribution networks

Overall business process, ease and efficiency

People aspect (those actually facilitating the delivery or providing support)

Productivity, the speed at which new services or functionality can be processed

Physical attributes, i.e. the appeal of services from a purely tangible and physical point of view.

Only by viewing strategic planning more from a tactical point of view, evolving every day as markets change, will airlines enable their staff and business model to deploy continual tactical moves that allow the attainment of corporate and more strategic goals and targets. A contemporary application of this can be through social media. Below, a case study is provided of KLM's use of social media as an illustration of one of the steps in the BPF methodology.

Case Study KLM and Social Media

One airline in particular has embraced social media as a key instrument in (re)engaging with customers, connecting with individuals to solve problems or be of assistance on a personal level, case by case, proactively. KLM Royal Dutch Airlines has been one of the most socially innovative airlines and currently employs 6 people that are working full-time and around the clock to monitor what people broadcast publicly, both in terms of travel-related issues and ideas or requests as broadcast by their clientele. The case study below describes how they do it:

"When it comes to social media case studies, airlines often prove to have some of the most impressive, influential and trendsetting results. Yet, despite all of the data that supports the adoption of innovative social media marketing initiatives for airlines, few seem to be as willing to go the distance as KLM[xxii].

KLM's social media program is brilliant...and they know it. When it comes to converting social media fans into paying customers, KLM is among the most successful brands around. In fact, on the KLM Facebook page, there is a section that breaks down their social media campaigns, explains how they went about executing them and posts the results. Effectively, they are their own social media case study as to why social is important to business. But our focus is a little deeper than that when it comes to our weekly case study. We aim to pull out the lessons marketers can learn from the KLM social media program as a whole.

The Campaigns

Featured on the KLM Facebook page are seven of their most successful social media campaigns. These campaigns include everything from "KLM Surprise" whereby special gifts would be presented to passengers who checked into flights using Foursquare or Twitter, to the "KLM Tile & Inspire" campaign whereby Facebook fans were asked to convert their Facebook profile picture into a Delft Blue tile and complete that tile with an inspiring message to be used as part of a mosaic design on a KLM aircraft that would travel across the globe.

Each campaign was equally inspired and generated similar results. For the two campaigns above, KLM reaped some considerable social benefits. The breakdown of the two featured campaigns by the numbers is below:

KLM Surprise Analytics

Foursquare	17528 followers
YouTube	154,722 views
Twitter	1597 followers
Tweet reach	2,6 million

KLM Tile & Inspire Analytics

Created tiles: 120000

Number of countries where tiles were created: 154

Views of the 2 videos: 1.3 million

Number of destinations the 777 flew to: 23

While the analytics are impressive enough as it is, the fact that KLM went on to further convert many of these fans is all the more notable. But what we wish to focus on is what KLM did that was as innovative and bold as it was simple and calculated.

The Lessons

Be Bold (But the Right Way)

KLM has had a far-from-conventional approach to their social media program. From presenting new meal options using Facebook videos that introduce the "chefs" (the "KLM A La Carte" campaign) to the controversial "KLM Meet and Seat" campaign that gave passengers the ability to preview their seat mates based on social profiles, KLM has dared to be innovative with each of their social media campaigns. But it is important to keep something in mind: the marketing execs at KLM knew exactly what they were doing, and these risks were as calculated as any.

By understanding the lead-to-conversion process, the KLM executives were able to put these campaigns together by using careful market research. Also, they amalgamated and improved data from their own failed exploits, discussed below, and from a clear understanding of the sales process for both the customer and the brand. You don't garner new customers from social media by doing the same thing as everyone else (hence, the "Be Bold" part of the lesson), but you certainly won't find them if you scare them away (and that covers the "Right Way" aspect). Thus, keep in mind that for a social media campaign to work, you need to impress your audience and to have the data to support your seemingly daring decisions.

Never Be Afraid to Try Something New

Social media is still in its infancy, and social media marketing even more so. There is no shortage of innovation out there, and with the ever-changing landscape of social media, you should never be afraid to be first to market. Your first-mover advantage will be huge when people see you doing something that no one has done before. KLM understands that and they have capitalized on it at every turn.

CRUISING TO PROFITS
Transformational Strategies for Sustained Airline Profitability

The airline only jumped into social media in 2009, but in these short few years they have managed to try their hand at virtually every campaign available on social media. Whether it is a Facebook campaign, a Foursquare promotion, a YouTube contest, or a Twitter "Live Reply" campaign wherein the airline responded to user tweets using up to 140 REAL people to spell out the message, you should never be afraid to try something that has never been done before. When it comes to social media, people want something they have not yet seen.

Try, Fail, Fix, Repeat

No one knows failed experiments better than KLM. Sure, they might have the budgetary luxury of making these mistakes, but over time they have learned exactly what they should not be doing in order to perfect their social campaigns. And on a smaller scale, you should never be afraid of the mistakes you make when it comes to social media. As we noted above, this is an incipient form of marketing; people are bound to make mistakes. But when you do, note your errors, redraft your campaign taking that into account, and start again.

For KLM, one of their big blunders came in 2011 when they offered a promotional gift to the first 50 male and first 50 female "Likers" of a post. Within minutes they had 1,500 "Likes" and no way of knowing which had come when. Oops! But what is important is that KLM recognized their mistakes, fixed them and, more importantly, accepted their failures. And that brings us to our final lesson.

Humility is an Underrated Trait

People appreciate humility. It is a humanizing trait, particularly when it comes from a company as large and reputable as KLM. That is why the last important lesson to pull from KLM is that, while you might be a big brand, social media is a place for you to simply be a voice in the conversation. While an image needs to be maintained, you can be a little less corporate and little more fun when it comes to social (respecting professional boundaries, of course). As we never tire of pointing out, social media is about exactly that: being social. Not only does KLM have a post on their blog detailing some of their yearly bloopers, but they also make an important point in their step-by-step guide on running their social media program:

"Not that campaigns always need to be global and spectacular. Many of our establishments have successfully launched their local pages, and we've learned that the power often lies in simplicity — like showing the interior of a cockpit, or thanking someone for notifying us about broken lighting on our KLM sign. Our creative editorial board delivers a daily dose of captivating, engaging posts through our various channels.

"Social campaigns have won us several awards, but it hasn't been one success after the next. We've certainly had our share of bloopers. But rather than hushing them up, we decided to make them public and take them as a learning experience. And as it turned out, people liked us even more for it."

The final step in the BPF framework revolves around the recognition that in many organizations, including airlines, a great deal of valuable knowledge about customers, markets, competition, and the internal workings and effectiveness of the airline, exists "out there," but is typically not used to its full potential. A number of techniques will be shared in the second part of *Cruising to Profits*.

By embedding analytics, intelligence, observations, experiences, and ideas, into a feedback loop in a structured way, it is arguably feasible to have strategy creation, formulation, and adjustment happen every day.

Chapter 9
Generation "C" and
Democratized Innovation

Social Media and Airline Marketing

Facebook, Myspace, LinkedIn, Plaxo, MSN, YM; these are some of the highly recognized names of an Internet era that revolves around people and exchanges. They are now commonly referred to as "social networks." Social networks have been described as "an Internet-facilitated and consumer-driven movement of networks, content and knowledge" built in web-based media tools that enable individuals to connect online[xxiii]. They increasingly spur a drastic need for marketing integration and/or a more fundamental integration of business functions and business processes around customer touchpoints, as described in this section.

Initially, many in the airline business considered social networking a fad that would fade away as new Internet platforms and types of communities would evolve. Some people argued that social networking and consumer-driven content and commentary on (un)official websites was no different than the old days of people calling customer service lines to complain about bad service, unfriendly service, or the quality of meals and bag handling service and claims. Posting comments on airline blogs, websites, and aviation chat rooms was often considered nothing more than noise and bad word-of-mouth carrying somewhat further and being more visible because it was public, prompting some airlines to attempt to control the bad press. Interestingly, it tended to be predominantly negative, as if customers needed to get something off their chest. It is the public and viral nature of social media that encouraged companies and airlines to be more responsive to and controlling of customer issues.

Now, there is something fundamental to social networking that has made it such a recent success with thousands, and then millions joining the bandwagon. Many airline managers now discover the potential power of this movement and that they need to adopt social networking before it starts to reflect poorly on airline marketing.

When considering what else persuaded airlines to get on board with social media, it is interesting to note that it was primarily driven by two things: (1) They wanted to know how to build their businesses; and (2) they wanted an edge on their competitors. For companies that wanted to grow, there was a rich opportunity to get the intelligence from customers and provide the service the customer wants.

Customers do not review social media as a complete replacement for voice and e-mail, but a powerful and convenient new channel of choice. Given the dominance or power of crowds, this will increasingly be so. For companies, this spells into a balancing act of resources and expertise among the various contact channels, but the online media demand the highest level of immediacy and responsiveness. Creating a single ace, competence, able to navigate through the resources they need — this is the requirement confronting them.

There has never been a better time for marketers to see, understand, and respond to the customer journey. Today's open social age has created a "looking glass" for companies to understand the complex nature of their customers, as millions of them are broadcasting their opinions, attitudes, behaviors, experiences and even unmet needs on a real-time basis.

In fact, society is rapidly approaching a complete digital state. New technologies have transformed the way people work, learn, communicate, and share. Also, consumers freely share their opinions and experiences on social networks, blogs, micro-blogs, message boards, forums, mainstream news sites and a variety of other online platforms.

According to Dimensional Research, over 90 percent of these consumers rely (to some extent and not exclusively) on independent reviews of products and services before they make a purchasing decision. Thus consumers trust perfect strangers, one can conclude.

Generation "C" — the Connected Traveler

While many within the marketing realm point to the customer journey fragmenting between the offline and online worlds, the mobile revolution is actually pulling these worlds more closely together than ever before. No longer are customers tethered to their computers. Today they are "always connected" to an array of shopping tools and social sources, empowering them and driving the era of the empowered customer.

In fact, according to a Morgan Stanley study, 91 percent of mobile users keep their device within three feet of them 24 hours per day. Mobile devices are now widely a standardization of life; people watch TV with them, make medical decisions with them and certainly shop with them.

This "always connected" state that mobile online accessibility facilitates is particularly transforming the way we all undertake traditional offline shopping activities, from conducting product comparisons and identifying best prices to locating coupons or offers and getting opinions and reviews. This, along with the all-time accessibility of mobile devices has made the wealth of information ubiquitous in the "offline" world.

A Versatile Journey

The empowerment consumers have with this information access presents a challenge for marketers to keep pace with the journey, which is ever changing. The inundation of information creates a myriad of paths customers can take toward their purchase. This wealth of information also increases the velocity of purchase decisions, often compressing the time between demand moments and decision points, making it even more challenging for marketers to identify and influence the purchase.

The key to driving success for marketers is to deeply understand consumers, continually map the journey and leverage this insight to drive messaging, education, promotions and innovation to align with the customers' needs (met and unmet) and wants. This requires business functions that interact or impact on end customers to align and share information so that it can be turned into customer intelligence that can be actionable.

Understanding the Journey

The basis for understanding the customer journey today is mapping it with advanced social intelligence. To adequately accomplish this it must be derived from the "big data" mining of millions of daily consumer social conversations. This appears simple in concept, but is very challenging in technical execution. This is why so many leading brands are turning to advanced, streaming "big data" solutions to deliver deep market and customer insights on a rapid basis.

The ability to analyze millions of customers and prospects allows for deep insights and the construction of key strategic journey components, which enables the organization to strategically drive decisions and innovation. Specifics within these types of detailed segments provide great value to the brand's ability to strategically message, promote and ultimately drive sales.

Along the same lines, using advanced social intelligence, the customer journey and particularly the critical path-to-purchase can be mapped to detail the specific demand moments and decision points driving the final purchase decision.

Many marketers think that this path-to-purchase mapping is only relevant to larger ticket items, like cars or electronics, due to the array of features and options and higher prices. While the customer journey is very relevant toward helping to influence these types of purchases, they are very applicable to low-ticket items as well, as the purchase decisions around trip planning are driven by an underlying purpose of the trip (derived purchases can be made, and they relate to components of the trip).

As an example, the path-to-purchase for trip planning includes a variety of steps many consumers go through in their decision process even for a low-priced trip. These steps range from surface transportation to entertainment options and ticket prices, to seasonal weather patterns, safety and violence considerations, to lifestyle aspects such as shopping options. It demonstrates that the ancillary approach of flight/hotel/car rental is overly simplistic in the airline world. Airlines can also be more helpful in destination planning for customers that travel for pure leisure and experience purposes. This would be like the concierge service explained in Volume 2 – The Practical Guide.

Today, with advanced social intelligence, accurately personifying customers and mapping their journey's has never been easier, more accurate or powerful. Leading corporations are adopting this methodology to drive their product innovation, packaging, messaging, promotions, positioning, placement, and ultimately their bottom line, by delivering what the consumer wants based on their own requests, interests, activities and attitudes.

FedEx Case Study

The Bigger the Brand, the bigger the social media strategy it seems, but we want to share a case study we picked up that provides a good illustration of how social media can engage customers.

Below is a case study[xxiv] of what FedEx does to delight its customers through excellent and timely service. Many of the interactions nowadays are happening through social channels.

In 2009, FedEx started working very closely with the marketing team to enhance the great brand of FedEx through the use of social media not just for marketing purposes, but for customer service as well. Following that decision the teams have seen amazing results. Providing a variety of channels for the customers to engage through, whether it's a phone, a chat, a blog or social networks like Facebook and Twitter, appeared to be highly beneficial. Even though FedEx does online listening, the marketing team is the one responsible for handling actionable requests that customer care follow-up to help solve the issue or answer the question. Their engagement time is mostly a matter of minutes, not hours or days. The team tracks online buzz and digital conversations through the internal score card that shows daily interactions with "authors" (FedEx team refers to their customers that create content and initiate conversations online as "authors") and what types those interactions were, as well as how fast the team responded. The FedEx approach affects brand perception and the bottom line, as is seen when observing some of their customers.

Nicole Snow is one perfect example of a now loyal customer. Snow owns a small business in Maine, called "Darn Good Yarn." She is in a remote area with few shipping options and extreme weather compounds her ability to run her home business. One day she reached out to FedEx on social networks and asked for help in getting her supply chain set up. The team responded immediately and helped her solve the problem. It did not seem like anything out of the ordinary, but that is incorrect.

A year later FedEx ran their first $25,000 small business grant contest which Ms. Snow won. She maintained the relationship with FedEx all that time, being a loyal customer. A year later, with the money she won, she was able to expand her business into new areas.

The case study from FedEx does provide us some pointers such as that it is necessary to integrate the interaction model across multiple functions (departments), as this speeds up the response and helps communicating a message that is consistent. The study also demonstrates that it pays to be genuine and authentic, and that it is important to delivery excellent service to each customer irrespective of their loyalty status. Part of this authentic approach is also the empowerment to try new things and take initiative in order to solve customer issues. However, adopting this style requires great discipline and scale in a high-volume business.

Democratizing Innovation

To many, innovation is a buzzword and has lost some of its value in everyday life. Innovation refers to "novelty" or "modernization," "advancement," "originality," and "improvement," and is increasingly of key importance in differentiating yourself as a company from the mainstream operators in the field. In the airline industry, this is a difficult task due to the commonality around the hard components of flight operations (airports, aircraft, and interiors). Still, innovation is required and demonstrates to loyal customers that the airline is investing in the well-being they experience and choices they have. Also, the need for innovation never ends, not even temporarily. Innovation is a constant agenda of changes and enhancements, trial and errors.

If we do not innovate, we argue that others will. For instance, hotel brands are generally stronger than airline brands. They truly are this way. Also, hotels have regained strength in the years following 9/11. Hotels are focused on personalized services and preferences and consider the more individual needs, rather than generalized characteristics of market segments. Who says hotels may not take the lead and offer travel facilitation and integrate it into their offering? Hotels and hotel chains could become the event and travel organizers and evolve into the online communication (human interaction and transportation) and well-being (wellness) facilitators. At least travel planning will finally be arrival-time-based and will allow more efficient flight shopping.

Democratizing innovation is about involving the customer in the process of modernizing the products and use of services. As users and customers, customers have great ideas. Few airlines recognize the value of customer feedback and ideas and incorporate them in product development. However, there is significant value in structuring the information and intelligence that is now available from direct channels (customer service/complaints or suggestions) and social media (both direct and indirect/public). We can only think of one airline that has formally launched a campaign (called "ThinkUp") to integrate customer feedback. Most recently, it asked customers for ideas on what the airline's new tablet experience should look like.[xxv]

Each time a person travels, the purpose of travel may be slightly different, even though the destination appears to be the same. The personal needs for certain types of services, amenities or even for the delivery of services during the travel cycle may change. It is very important to capture this level of detail, which can only come from direct input from the customer her/himself. Also, how fare products and offerings can be unbundled and repackaged should be driven by insights from the customers. By aggregating details obtained at a micro-segment, e.g. the individual level, clear patterns should become visible, and as a result the airlines are able to design their service offerings more in line with personalized needs and lifestyle profiles. It is also important to highlight that personal preference can vary by season and destination, direction (East/West, or North/South), number of time zones to cross, aircraft type, and so forth. It can be very granular and complex.

Disparity

There is one challenge facing all companies with regards to social media in that there are so many disparate channels in which they are expected to participate that it becomes very challenging, time-consuming, and expensive to manage the whole. And oftentimes, it is not a directly revenue-producing effort but rather just living up to customer expectations. Consider an airline that communicates to the public and is forced to post in the following channels:

RSS Feeds:

AIRLINEX press releases: www.AirlineX.com/rss.asp?a=press
AIRLINEX news: http://www.AirlineX.com/rss.asp?a=news
AIRLINEX events: http://www.AirlineX.com/rss.asp?a=events

Social Networks:

Web: www.AirlineX.com
Blog: http://blog.AirlineX.com
Twitter: http://twitter.com/AIRLINEX
Facebook: www.facebook.com/AIRLINEX

LinkedIn: www.linkedin.com/company/AIRLINEX-
YouTube: www.youtube.com/user/AIRLINEX
SlideShare: www.slideshare.net/AIRLINEX

The final step in the BPF framework revolves around the recognition that in many organizations, including airlines, a great deal of valuable knowledge exists, about customers, markets, competition, and the internal workings and effectiveness of the airline, but that needs to be shared and fed back in a structured way in order to have internal value. This also could support a proper alignment between the various departments and ultimately the delivery of the value proposition around which the business model is built. Our proprietary techniques in the area of daily strategy formulation and restoration will be shared in part in the next book, **Cruising to Profits**, Volume 2 – The Practical Guide.

As society is rapidly approaching a complete digital state, and new technologies and platforms — such as social media — transform the way people work, learn, communicate and share, there has never been a better time for marketers to see, understand and respond to the customer journey.

CRUISING TO PROFITS

Transformational Strategies for Sustained Airline Profitability

Chapter 10
Applying BeProFit
(Segmentation)

At the heart of the **Cruising to Profits** business transformation methodology is the approach to the role of commercial aviation in the world's economy and in peoples' lives. By default, and by proposing to reconsider the scale or overall size of the industry to profitably fit this role, we have taken a constructive view of the customer base and of the need to more carefully segment the market. In this chapter, I apply our business model optimization tool and assess how two key components in business models (customers, and customer segments) influence and impact on the other components. While not all techniques are revealed in this chapter, they will be available in Volume 2.

Frequent Flyers: Loyalty Redefined

One of the successful trends in customer management since the 1980s has been the use of Frequent Flyer Programs (FFPs) to reward travelers for their business with airlines, in an attempt to create captive audiences that would reduce travel on competing airlines. The FFPs became widely popular because of the many perks associated with the various membership tiers, which translates mainly into ego-stroking and recognition-based practices, although important benefits, related to ease of travel and a speedy airport and airplane boarding process, exist. While the FFPs are called "Loyalty Programs," they are essentially captive marketing programs that aim to influence customer choice by imposing implicit obstacles to switching carriers, especially in markets where carriers compete directly (e.g., non-stop direct service between city pairs). These obstacles do not necessary relate to a superior or premium core product in today's business models.

While frequent flyers, as defined by airlines, clearly travel more often than the average traveler, the benefit for airlines is that it represents incremental revenue per known customer but does not necessarily translate in incremental profitability. The argument that a frequent traveler is a more profitable traveler for the airline is almost without exception incorrect. High-status frequent travelers often still expect the lowest available fare and frequently displace other passengers using accumulated miles/credits that would otherwise have been a revenue seat by a paying customer, even with the rules airlines put in place regarding the availability of those seats. Thus a clear trade-off is involved. However, we have often seen that the frequency with which a passenger travels with a given airline seemingly provides a psychological comfort level of business predictability. And this is false, as one cannot bank on it, given the number of factors that determine carrier choice.

Also, it is important to remember that brands do not offer loyalty; people grant it to the brand. Customers are human, and loyalty is an emotion. Given the diverse mix of people, personalities and personal needs and wants (also at a psychological level), no technology will get close enough to tell or predict us what customers want and what they do not want. Research can provide insights, but little guidance, when it comes to real-time product/service offering at a personalized level consistently across all entry points, channels, and touchpoints. In fact, the development of loyalty is not getting easier with time; it is only becoming more complex.

Employees are also human and they also affect customers, and how an employee engages with customers can or will ultimately affect the bottom line of an airline. Therefore, there is a strong case to be made for the segmentation of employees, not only customers. This is further discussed in Volume II of this book.

Managing Loyalty, Not Loyalty Programs

The FFPs have become monsters of complexity and arguably have taken a life of their own, with an increasing lack of focus on the actual customers that drive the very activity of FFPs. The move to merchandising has only propelled this issue. It is so tempting to get bogged down in the intricacies and technicalities of loyalty programs, that in the end the customer's traveling experience gets somewhat ignored. But there is a clear need to redefine the approach to FFPs and a need to start managing loyalty, not loyalty programs.

That entails a refocus on people, as the granting of loyalty or the indifferent behavior are fundamentally human emotions.

Brands do not Create Loyalty — People *Grant Loyalty to the Brand*

Where loyalty management falls short in the aviation sector is at the transactional level, at the purchase of the ticket. Also, many travelers would assume that loyalty should be rewarded by discounts. But we, like many marketing experts, warn that, among other dangers, premium brands offering loyalty mainly through discounts and travel and merchandise credits could potentially harm loyalty and destruct profit margins. Ultimately, it may lead to a decline in brand value, which is a trend we observed in the US-domestic market.

Advances in technology have made FFPs more effective, accurate, and appealing to clients, but the advances in technology have also made it easier for customers to compare and switch companies, and new companies have sprung to life betting on creating value in this field. People can compare stock prices, airline tickets and related services and price outlays at the click of a mouse.

To fully realize the potential of their loyalty schemes, suppliers in the travel, hospitality, and transportation industries must be flexible, responsive, innovative, and cost-efficient. The loyalty scheme must be able to maximize the benefits for all key stakeholder groups, that is, the host airline, members and partners. The current generation of loyalty systems falls short of supporting these goals, due to a limited scope and focus that does no longer reflect today's industry. Next generation Customer Relationship Management products will be unique in their ability to meet travel and transportation business needs for a complete, powerful and flexible platform for loyalty management optimization and member satisfaction. This CRM component, which is part of "C" (customers) and "CS" (customer segments) in business model optimization, needs to be integrated in the overall business system that handles the transactions we complete with customers.

It is important to remember that people are not as predictable as technology. One thing may make one person more loyal while upsetting another. Or worse, something that fosters loyalty one day may not be perceived as desirable the next day.

Segmentation must be related to personal identity and personal preference, which are fluid. It varies by date, season, origin-destination combination, and even direction of travel (e.g., East-to-West vs. West-to-East, daytime vs. night time). This personalization requires the customer's input, which can be referred to as "open segmentation" or "democratized innovation".

A modern look at the overall segmentation as well as customer relationship management and FFPs dictates an aligned approach around the following pillars:

Personal recognition

Whether a client is traveling for business purposes (in Business Class or Economy Class) or personal purposes, it is the same customer with typically the same preferences;

however, the overall customer treatment is highly dependent on old-fashioned classifications of people. Loyalty is about recognition and the provision of a responsive match to customer needs that serves both the consumer and the brand.

Personalization

Frequent travelers do not like to be grouped into categories and increasingly want control over the travel component of their overall purpose of travel, during the booking as well as the traveling phase, up to and including service amenities and timing.

The basic premise is that successful delivery on expectations and on customer experience requires specific input from each customer with regard to their preferences. This requires active exchanges between the airline and the customer. A new business process could be designed around not just how personal preferences are learned, but also incorporated into offerings when prompted by shopping.

It is important for airlines to realize that the customer may not want to purchase air transportation, but might want to purchase instead a facilitative service related to communication (any means by which conducting business or personal connections can be enhanced) or well-being, as identified earlier. For instance, a customer may be interested to deal exclusively with the airline for his/her telephony and internet connectivity requirements throughout the person's network and travel requirements around the world. There is no reason airlines could not occupy this space.

Relevancy

Campaigns organized by general marketing that include the target group maintained by frequent flyer programs need to be cleansed for relevancy and targeted offers. This especially applies to merchandising or partner programs such as those from financial institutions (e.g. credit card membership offers) to those people that are in the distribution group but already hold these products or use these services.

Technology savvy

From a technology point of view, in recent years travel and hospitalities have made significant improvements in terms of Customer Relationship Management (CRM), using enhanced business technology that boosts functionality, hence allowing marketers to better segment and target their markets with individualised offers. Especially with the use of technology and the maintenance of customer data bases, airlines should know sufficiently about each customer when they log into the portals (e.g., booking/reservation or the FFP) to customize the presentation of offerings to those that are relevant and could appeal to the person that is logging in. Too often we find a blanket approach to campaigns, leading to campaigns that are ill-targeted.

Let me try to tie what I described above back into the business model discussion. While loyalty programs have traditionally focussed on encouraging customer loyalty, repeat business, and a steady flow of revenue, many organizations still view loyalty management as a support function that has little interaction with other marketing functions. As such, loyalty management often finds itself in relative isolation, with limited opportunities to innovate within the larger marketing domain. Even in today's "always-connected" world, many loyalty programs do not resonate with their members. Several cases provide evidence that the fragmentation and disconnect of vital marketing insights is at the core of the problem, with 94 percent of marketers surveyed saying they do not consistently apply insights[xxvi] — such as an individual's long-term value or social influence and attitude — to create meaningful engagements.

The challenge is that loyal customers are not one of a kind, thus crafting reward products that are bundled as a value proposition that makes sense to each individual is complex. Some programs offer frequent fliers to select certain benefits, once having qualified for a specific tier level.

Companies lament about challenges in using data to listen to the customer. Today's disparate data sets have magnified the difficulty of matching current and future needs, wants and interests of the customer in a timely manner. The abundance of data holds great promise but makes it difficult to truly understand consumers' current desires.

In this chapter, I apply our business model optimization tool and assess how two key components in business models (customers, and customer segments) influence and impact on the other components. Loyalty is not defined by frequency of travel, and we contend that the focus should shift from managing loyalty programs to managing loyalty.

A modern look at segmentation and customer relationship management dictates an aligned approach around the pillars of (1) personal recognition, (2) personalization, (3) relevancy, and (4) technology. The chapter concludes that the value proposition at the heart of the business model must consistently deliver across all touchpoints for all services in all circumstances related to the derived nature of demand. Redesigning an airline around the latter requirement will prepare it to weather the inescapable business model life cycles as well as economic cycles.

Chapter 11

Implications of BeProFit on Revenue Optimization

One of the areas of key interest for the application of the **BeProFit** framework is Revenue Management. Often defined as the functional area of which the primary aim is selling the right product to the right customer at the right time for the right price, it has typically been a back-office analytics-based business function that is not well integrated in the overall business model, in the overall commercial and delivery business process of airlines or in other functional areas. Let me explore this in some detail and apply the BeProFit framework to assess the results.

RM and Business Model Integration

When the practice of Revenue Management (RM) became more widespread and popular in the late 1980s, but especially in during the 1990s, the focus always was predominantly on inventory control[xxvii] and differential pricing[xxviii]. However, traditionally the focus was on only one revenue component, i.e., the base fares in the pricing structure. Other fees, such as change fees or cross-selling and up-selling revenues were not considered as part of the RM processes that increasingly became supported by automated system support. The software packages that came onto the market were mainly focused on demand forecasting based on historical demand patterns and the allocation of authorized selling capacities for each subset (micro segment) of demand as controlled by inventory "buckets" or booking classes.

A number of fundamental changes have occurred in the airline industry that challenged the traditional RM models, specifically as new business models came to life. Some of the changes have been tackled with new approaches, business processes and software packages that address such variations from the traditional Full Service Carrier models. An example of this is the low-cost carrier approach to the abandonment of the fare restrictions (and thus the removal of the fences between traditional business vs. leisure traveler) by allowing any traveler access to low fares as long as they book early. The typical LCC booking curve is communicated simply as "the fare will continue to go up as the plane is filling up with reservations." This simplification and treatment of travelers as dependent demand created havoc with the software systems that had been designed using the differential pricing logic.

But more importantly, it became increasingly evident that RM was in fact an isolated area where we would find analysts working on and applying models without a thorough assessment of how RM impacts on or supports the overall Business Model Optimization (BMO). Considering the illustration below again, key questions arise:

How does RM support key customer segments as identified as crucial in the business model?

How does RM support the relationship building and management with key customers?

How does RM apply effectively through all the customer purchase channels?

How is RM logic communicated at all touchpoints where customers shop for products and services?

How does RM impact on the optimal cost structure as identified in the business model?

What are the incremental costs of applying RM logic and systems to the business?

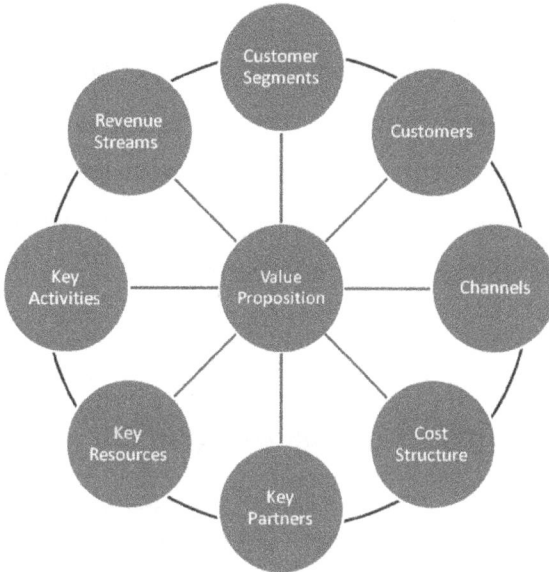

How does RM impact on the relationships with key partners (e.g. alliances)?

Does RM logic maintain a balanced "win-win" ethic with commercial partners?

How does RM impact on the key resources that have been identified as critical success factors in BMO?

How does RM fit into the key activities that are the lifeblood of the airline?

How does RM generate and contribute to the key revenue streams that are essential to the company?

How do immediate benefits outweigh the foregone revenue or turned away business?

But most importantly: how effective is RM in the core consistent value proposition of the airline?

The questions below become ever so difficult to answer when we attempt to answer them from an overall business process perspective that requires all activities to logically and smoothly transit customers from value proposition to booking to experience management.

RM and Business Process Integration

Ultimately, everything culminates in the value proposition that is made to customers and how the service offering is perceived and experienced. It again brings commercial engagement (what is presented / offered / promised) and delivery (how it is used / experienced / perceived) closely together at the heart of Business Model Optimization.

It is as such of paramount importance that RM be lifted from the analytical corner and be made part of an overall commercial optimization process that fits into the more holistic Business Model Optimization process. RM has profound impact on the availability or accessibility of the core product and related services or components thereof.

CRUISING TO PROFITS
Transformational Strategies for Sustained Airline Profitability

Therefore, all sacrifices (all chargeable items/prices and cash outlays) and rewards (service components) need to be considered in a framework that can be communicated well to the travelers. That framework also needs to communicate the costs related to flight operations on short and long distances and how costs differ when operating small versus large wide-body aircraft. There is no reason not to educate the public.

As a result, educating the public requires the framework that communicates:

> A rationalized fare structure that is better aligned with costs;
> Air fares as they relate to the costs of operating different types of flight missions;
> The economics of operating large aircraft with dense seating over long distances;
> The base fare, as well as all applicable taxes (they matter to the customer);
> Change fees (and appropriateness of such fees relative to the inconveniences caused to airlines)
> Up-sell fees (upgrades and premium services)
> Cross-sell fees (ancillary revenues from merchandising).

From a customer perspective, all products and services that have an associated price or non-financial cost need to be integrated in a more all-encompassing business process that is intuitive and smooth to process people through as supported by RM. RM does require a customer-smarter approach that is not considered punitive and can be communicated more effectively as value-added for customers. Travelers understand airlines need to make money, but the process through which that is handled today is very opportunistic and communicated very poorly in terms of offering presentation throughout the various channels. In fact, it is not communicated consistently through the various channels such as websites, tablet/smartphone Apps or other mobile devices.

In addition, the RM practices today mainly consider revenues from air transportation and air travel-related aspects, but do not yet include ground-based services and value-added components other than the standard car rental and hotel accommodation as well as insurance options.

RM and (Other) Functional Integration

Integrating RM more effectively in the overall business process of an airline requires it to be more aligned with and integrated into other business functions. Specifically, it brings me back to the point where I raise our key BMO question: **Where lies the overall customer ownership, offer and experience management?**

Due to the fact that RM impacts on all of the core business model components, as depicted above, it is clear that it is difficult to maintain an "independent" RM department. While we need RM specialists, they need to be integrated in and working with all other existing business functions today, such as sales, marketing, product management, alliance management, CRM, loyalty/FFP, flight operations, finance, and human resources.

Illustration of Functional Integration (CRM and RM)

Let me consider a more specific example of a much-needed integration, between just two areas, that of CRM and RM.

Even though in theory CRM and RM are areas that should be compatible, in many ways they are currently not. As exposed in the table below, while revenue management is mainly concerned with short-term revenue optimization based on controlling product availability among customers grouped by broad characteristics, customer relationship management is aimed at attaining overall marketing effectiveness through the recognition of preferences of specific individuals.

Also, both CRM and RM possess key marketing information that represents significant actionable value, should an exchange be made available. Loyalty management does not typically have access to reservations data or invaluable demand forecasts. Furthermore, it is not kept abreast of potential available inventory that could be made available for redemption or other marketing promotions. For instance, airline frequent flyer programs could promote redemption travel or tailor-made promotions for flights and markets flagged by revenue management as lagging.

In addition, a key discrepancy between RM and CRM is the market orientation of segments versus the potential micro-segments (individuals). Revenue management is predominantly concerned with optimizing the availability of products across market segments through the use of classes or revenue buckets. However, loyalty management has the potential ability to recognize each individual's tastes and preferences and propose personalized product bundles based on utility and willingness to pay. The tremendous value of the latter is generally not compatible with optimization techniques applied by revenue management.

Evidently, the ultimate success and profitability of CRM lies in the opportunity to capitalize on each member's preferences in terms of products, product features, and flexibility. At the same time, it becomes increasingly important to close the gap on customer value, his/her willingness to pay, and the availability of preferred products at a time that matches the customer's value and the economic shelf value of that product at that time.

The above describes what is often dubbed "customer-centric" marketing, supported by revenue management. It necessitates a fully integrated approach of marketing (including product development) and RM, and is another example of business model, process and functional integration approach (**BeProFit**).

In the future, it will be increasingly important to view each customer as a micro segment and move from a transaction-based sales model to personalized offerings around individual customer profitability. That should be based on both short-term (an infrequent) and long-term (very frequent) customers. This will be the first step in moving from today's Revenue Management to full business-model-based commercial optimization supported by marketing science.

The challenge today, given that we live in an era of increasing automation / software / technology-enabled processes, is that our reality presents a case in point that legacy technology has become an impediment to change. This is particularly true for the replacement of existing technology that has emotional value to those that were involved in the initial development and maintenance.

But new decision-making support solutions are required to support business model optimization and facilitate functional integration. This integration will help create the overall business process that is consistent and delivers customized services based on market segmentation and differentiation.

There are some causes for concern as the industry evolves and the RM discipline is not following suit in addressing the overall decision-making support requirements that would allow a more comprehensive and appropriate commercial optimization.

Second, existing RM systems are not fully embedded in commercial sales business processes, in that they operate on a disparate basis, run and calibrated by RM analysts that are not directly involved in the day-to-day operations or sales process, let alone loyalty management or first-line customer contact at airports. This has created an isolated and alienated departmental approach, which has never really been addressed or rectified through proper change management integration. In this approach, the tools were the focus, not the overall business process and the overarching business objective. In fact, this situation has led to confusion and internal (sub-optimal) conflict.

A fundamental question is therefore to what extent the current business model applied to sales and operations is a desirable one in the longer run, particularly as we can expect increasing levels of input costs driven by regulatory requirements (security and customs among others), but especially capital costs (modern fleet requirements to capitalize on fuel efficiencies) and the cost of fuel itself.

This requires us to look at the industry differently and play by different rules, and thus requires us to take a fresh look at the systems and decision-support tools we are using, and especially at their underlying assumptions. But more importantly, it requires us to refocus on the overall business model and business process we want new systems to support. The latter implies all systems that support the sale and operation of air transportation over a global network in a commercially optimized manner.

This all seems too large to be practical, to grasp, or to achieve due to the intrinsically political and cross-border challenges that exist today. But focusing on market share and a pure air transport or flight-driven culture has failed to deliver true economic returns that can weather economic instability.

A noteworthy opportunity exists to introduce a systematic approach to revenue optimization, supported by business technology consisting of decision-making as well as automated optimization tools, using our framework for transformational strategies for sustained profitability, consisting of (1) business model optimization, (2) alignment of business functions to business model components, (3) alignment and integration of business functions, and (4) embedding value-creation strategy formulation in day-to-day activities. This was described in the previous chapter in more detail.

Customer-Centric Offering & Revenue Optimization

There is tremendous merit in moving from transaction-driven activities to customer-centric optimization. The term "customer-centric" appears to be gradually replaced by "personalization" but essentially they encapsulate the same. We are referring again to the unbundling of all flight-related features and services in order to allow customers to pick-and-choose those items they consider of value, and for which they are willing to pay.

Consider this example. If you fly Business Class on an eastbound (night time) transatlantic flight, you may require a flat bed and a light or express meal. You may want to have access to your e-mail or Internet for the first two hours of the flight. If you fly Business Class on a westbound (day-time) transatlantic flight, you may not require a bed, and no alcoholic beverages. You may want leg room, work space, and indeed, access to e-mail, Internet, phone, and so forth. Today, that is not feasible yet. Can one conclude that the service offering is an inflexible commodity?

In Economy Class, people may be willing to pay two dollars for a nice pillow and blanket or choice of entertainment, movies. They may be willing to pay up to five dollars for the guarantee they do not get a middle seat. We are talking about only a few dollars. But just for comparison, if we, as an airline industry, had been able to charge up to 4 dollars per passenger more last year, the entire worldwide airline industry would have been profitable for a decade since September 11, 2001.

CRUISING TO PROFITS
Transformational Strategies for Sustained Airline Profitability

---

New technology and ultra-long-haul aircraft such as the Boeing 787 and 777LR will require a new approach to in-flight service. As a case in point, I may not have had time to study my entertainment options at destination. I may as well use the time in-flight to search and book theatre tickets, restaurants, trips to the Great Wall, and all other options. We could sell anything to this captive audience during an 18 hour flight. And they are likely to be requesting these services sooner than we think. Most watch movies out of pure boredom anyways.

Identifying what people want is the conventional task of marketing. But most of us are not integrating all information that can be obtained from our CRM, FFP, and web analytics systems in order to focus on individuals, rather than the wider clientele. Even Revenue Management systems are still processing numbers, not individuals. And most are still plied with the fundamental problem of fare products. People do not buy fare products; they buy a bundle of services that is of value to them. Restrictions, lack of flexibility, penalties, and the like, are sacrifices. Do we want their business or not? How would it make *you* feel?

Airline management could allow revenue management analysts to focus on overall and individual traffic numbers, booking behaviors, and profiles that are circumstance or event-driven. Deep analysis and deep or hybrid market segmentation are required. Each customer is a segment, let's face it, and this is just another case in point for business function alignment and value-creation strategy formulation in day-to-day activities, two key components of our transformational framework.

Evidently, this will require new tools, new systems. Some of us are working on them, and those that show the biggest interest are those that are industry leaders in our business. I suggest leaving the old approach to legacy channels, such as the current GDS. Not that they do not evolve, as they have been focusing on the next generation platforms that will allow deep and rich content, and will be concentrating on increasing the dollar value in each transaction through cross-selling and up-selling.

This chapter concludes that the traditional back-office analytics-based revenue management function is limited in relevancy in the wider and holistic business model optimization framework of **BeProFit**. It is found that a review of RM practices reveals that revenue optimization for maximized profits should not be aligned with the transactional-level air transportation purchase, but with the overall value proposition linked to the derived nature of the demand for air travel. We thus promote a much larger scope of activity and integration as part of the functional alignment techniques we have advanced.

By including other functional components of business model optimization in the scope of revenue optimization, a proper term for this practice is more likely commercial optimization. While many marketers speak of customer-centric strategies, in essence we propose to focus on value-proposition centric management by individual and customer segments.

Chapter 12
The Role of Business Technology

While this book in the **Cruising to Profits** series centers on presenting a business transformation methodology for sustained airline profitability, it is clear that the underlying concept and practical measures require not only changes in airline organization, but also in processes, as we have highlighted. The third component in facilitating this is related to information systems, currently more accurately referred to as business technology.

Implications of BPF Framework on Business Technology

In order to deliver a great passenger experience we have to personalize our service to match the passenger's experience. This is not easy with the many different solutions and technologies employed by the airline. It is a challenge to bring all these solutions together, from the passenger profile in the frequent flyer, to the check-in system to provide the preferred seat, to the catering system to prepare the desired meal, to the CRM solution to handle the passenger's feedback, and to link all of this to the travel history of the passenger. Providing consistent and personalised passenger service and experience depends on the tight, seamless integration between different systems and technologies. This is more challenging when one is taking a renewed look at existing business systems for overall business transformation, innovation, and strategic planning purposes.

Following the BPF framework by taking a wider perspective of commercial aviation's role in facilitating communication and well-being, it is evident that business technology will play a key role in allowing the industry to fully embrace the opportunities related to this paradigm. It entails an array of other aspects around the customer's original purpose for travel and true needs that could form an endless list of services. The challenge is to get access to and integrate these items in a user-friendly choice-based shopping and purchasing mechanism.

CRUISING TO PROFITS
Transformational Strategies for Sustained Airline Profitability

In its annual Airline IT Trends Survey, Airline Business/SITA identified a recent trend toward increased expenditure in consumer technologies.[xxix] The survey highlighted that 98 percent of those that participated are committing resources to delivering passenger services via mobile devices; 100 percent are investing in business intelligence; and overall IT expenditure will be up approximately 2.35 percent in 2013.

Among the key IT challenges mentioned in the above survey feature a number of items that appear to be in line with the underlying proposition of our **BeProFit** framework, notably the need for the alignment of business functions supporting the various business model components in order to perform business model optimization. Consider the following challenges that were mentioned:

Complexity of business and collaboration across teams
Influencing the business to think and act more strategically about IT and
 investment in systems
Business IT alignment, adapting IT to the growing business

Given the proposed business transformation approach I have put forward in this book, it is evident that this approach and management framework requires a fundamental look at the systems and software packages that are used to support decision-making and operational automation in today's world, and more importantly, that will be required in the future. Remarkably, the Airline Business/IT Survey also pinpointed that one of the major IT failures is the *"inability to [have] a single view of customers enterprise-wide"* and *"being unable to invest enough in breakthrough innovation."*

It is preferable to refer to business solutions or business systems rather than Information Technology or software, as many people believe that technology will increasingly become a business driver for change and allow the development and deployment of new business models that were not possible before without such technology. Not only are systems used to support operations and decision-making processes, but also they more and more enable firms to carve out new niches in certain market segments through new and moderns ways of targeting and reaching new customers through new channels (e.g., mobile) with innovative service products.

Re-positioning Technology

If we adhere to the framework we discussed earlier, the various components of our transformational approach stipulate the following:

Redefine the role of aviation

The scope of the systems has to widen to other sectors in which air transportation is included, to allow it to approximate the original demand from which the demand for air transport is derived. For example, planning systems need to look at wider trends in global trade, economic relations, trends in events and conferences as well as tourism, financial indicators (such as exchange rates), and ethnic communities and travel patterns, as well as governmental agencies' priorities and people movement around the world.

Rightsize the air transportation sector

Each carrier in the world is aware of the passengers they carry in terms of the passenger volume and total revenues it generates. What is a somewhat more difficult is to derive an accurate indication of the profit (or loss) that each passenger generates. While loyalty teams make attempts to calculate the lifetime values of frequent flyers, the industry is still predominantly concerned with top-level numbers (revenue, passenger counts, number of aircraft/departures/seats, and load factors). If the aviation sector is to behave as a commercial business, business systems will allow airlines to more accurately bring supply and demand in line and restructure their networks not around growth in production and market share but in profitability share.

Adopt transformational organizational strategies for sustained profitability

1) Business model optimization

The future in business systems that will support full business model optimization lies in a holistic approach to analytics, predictive analysis and commercial steering/optimization.

If one would be able to understand how the modus operandi of an airline can be broken down in the various business-model components that make up the paradigm and how one can establish interrelationships between inputs and outputs and correlate the performance in one area to profitability in another, it would be possible to create a true steering mechanism and cockpit-style approach to business-model management. It would help guide airlines to identify where the market opportunities and trends are, what customers to target and through which channels, and how to best package bundles of services that are personalized and include the customer's input through open innovation using social media, at the appropriate "sticky" price points that allow the airline to be profitable, considering its partners (alliances) and cost structure and limitations.

For instance, once airlines can offer uninterrupted internet access (through Wi-Fi) on board, there are opportunities to monetize an array of new service offerings, such as shopping, destination applications, event planning and arrangements, as well as gaming and "edutaining." [xxx]

2) Overlaying business functions on business model components

Today, it is not possible to map the various systems that are used in an airline to the business model components we outlined before. That is, one can only draw a chart manually, but there is no systematic way of identifying how departmental activities and the software they use relate to or correlate with the commercial health of each of the business model components. For instance, how do loyalty or FFP and the software they use correlate with the measurement of commercial success as it relates to key activities, partners, cost, and the likelihood of success of the overall value proposition. Can this be structured and automated?

One clear trend is that of driving customer engagement through mobility and self-service, and this trend cuts across the airline organization, in that a holistic approach is required in order to facilitate a flawless customer engagement and service delivery process.

"Our goal for IT strategy is to place customers at the heart of everything it does, to be connected to them throughout their journey and to be as efficient as possible in the way it serves them"
– Patrick O'Keeffe, VP Airline Operations Technology, American Airlines.

3) Aligning business functions

By the same token, in order to align business functions to business model components, it will be necessary to align or integrate the countless software packages or systems that are used in the numerous departments that exist today in a typical airline organization. While this may seem an unrealistic task, it will spell the difference between strategic repositioning and commercial success and the status quo of lingering struggles in the aviation sector. Also, with the appropriate leadership and persistence, this is feasible.

4) Embedding value-creation strategy formulation in day-to-day activities

Ideas are born when people have the opportunity to observe, reflect and make interpretations of what they see. In many functions or activities in an airline (whether it relates to operational or commercial activities), proper analytical systems and information-capture tools can breed a great deal of insight and business intelligence that can be converted into ideas that people can drive through initiatives.

Realigning Business Systems

Interfacing CRM to RM cannot be implemented in a plug-and-play manner due to the discrepancy in market focus. However, CRM can herald itself as an integrator of innovative marketing and segmentation, including revenue optimisation. This requires organizations to think and act differently. For instance, many marketing decision-makers do not seem to know how to optimally use the wealth of untapped RM data, analysis, and techniques. Similarly, revenue managers face system-related obstacles and inventory controls that impede the implementation of a differentiated customer-centric product offering and pricing scheme. This can only be overcome by integrating revenue management, pricing, reservations, and marketing into a function that could be termed "customer revenue and loyalty optimisation."

At a time when the discipline of revenue management is attempting to re-concentrate on the original goals and culture of its discipline, it is now opportune to implement the next generation of customer-value-based business technology that will be equally rewarding for customers and the travel and hospitality industries.

In conclusion, now that the industry's financial results appear to be strengthening, the timing is ripe to invest in sophisticated business management solutions so as to enjoy maximized profits.

Big or Small Data

In mid-2010, the information universe carried 1.2 zettabytes and 2020 predictions expect nearly 44 times more at 35 zettabytes coming our way. All this big data does not necessarily mean big insights for business. The only way for that is through powerful analytics and interactive reporting tools that deliver high performance results by keeping up with modern chip technology.

At the end of the day, aligning systems and processes to support business function-alignment or business model optimization all centers on the availability, processing and interpretation of data. Today, discussions on big data are plentiful but many companies are embarrassed about the quality of their data and the lack of proper use of such data. However, increasingly the experts in the field of analytics are vocal about the fact that waiting until all the data quality issues are resolved is a mistake, as the fundamental data requirements can often be satisfied. At the very least, it helps identifying the more refined needs and data requirements. Companies can then move from current data to data analysis to predictive analysis for decision-making support.

Predictive analytics is about projecting forward and transforming the company. While predictive analytics projects can require a substantial investment up front, return on investment studies show that it does make an impact. Ultimately, even small-scale projects can have an enormous impact on the bottom line. So while the risks are high, so are the rewards. One has to persist and follow through and act on what one learns.

But even more powerful is prescriptive analytics, which allows a marketer and manager to use powerful insights into which customers that are most likely going to stop being a customer or, conversely, those that would potentially use additional services and spend more provided they are "touched" by a company representative.

"Our client projects have demonstrated the tremendous power of prescriptive analytics when business managers act on our recommendations. We see significant differences in customer spend between customers that were touched versus those that were left untouched"

– Michael Foliot, President & CEO, TDT Business Solutions & Analytics.

Most companies have data residing in multiple data sources. The challenge is how to aggregate the data from legacy systems, different databases, excel spreadsheets and so forth. More importantly, it is important to ensure that data cleansing is done, eliminating missing and or duplicate entries, ensuring that values in fields correspond to what should be there. This can be a daunting task for anyone to undertake, but this first step is critical in understanding the data and subsequently conducting various predictive analyses. This activity is an integral part of the process we propose to our customers. That is, taking data from multiple data sources and creating a dataset that can then be data mined and analyzed.

Customer Analytics

Today, companies like airlines witness a vastly increased supply of information where they can aggregate years of research and development data into databases. Also, recent technical advances have made it easier to collect and analyze information from multiple sources – a major benefit. So when it comes to customer analytics, a lack of customer data is not the issue. Rather, it is what organizations do with this data. To gain a complete understanding of their customers, airlines need to turn data into insight, and action. They also need to present results in a meaningful way so the first responders can use them to improve service, personalize marketing and drive profitability.

However, it is still a complex task to move from data analysis to action and specific initiatives that accelerate value and innovation. Also, the value pathways evolve as new data become available, fostering a feedback loop, but complicating those attempting to correlate new data to existing analytics and patterns.

Aggregating individual data sets into big-data algorithms often provides the most robust evidence, since nuances in subpopulations (such as the presence of patients with gluten allergies) may be so rare that they are not readily apparent in small samples. Even a few simple interventions can have an enormous impact when scaled up.

Nevertheless, the data that is collected and analyzed has limited value if airline strategists and managers do not consider the wider perspective of the purpose and role of commercial aviation. The fundamental ideology or paradigm that one adopts around the airline business model will drive what data marketers are looking for and what they will consider in crafting new business models or variations thereof. Thus we maintain that the industry must undergo fundamental changes before stakeholders can capture its full value and the value of analytics.

Trending Toward Predictive Analytics

As the field of analytics is maturing more, it has identified the need to and progressed into more forward-looking techniques to help guide managers simulate business scenarios and make estimations and/or predictions of likely results of certain actions.

Out-of-The-Box Thinking is Out the Window

Increasingly, as airlines realize that mobility, self-service, cloud solutions allow them to differentiate their brands and increase their chances of monetization through new services/solutions, offered and delivered through new channels to newly attracted customers, their IT strategy will have to change. We believe that this will lead many airlines to rethink their IT strategy and will encourage them to embrace custom solutions more and more, as this differentiation requires a departure from standardized software packages. This will be discussed as one of the key components in a subsequent volume of the *Cruising to Profits* series. For instance, one strong advocator of low-cost and standardized software and technology packages (jetBlue) has now come out and publicly stated that among their top priorities features the move from out-of-the-box solutions to custom solutions.

By 2020, Chief Marketing Officers will be spending more on technology than Chief Information Officers. This chapter concludes that IT systems that traditionally supported functional areas or airline departments will become obsolete as organizations need to behave more holistically as integrated service companies dealing with individual customers.

Leading corporations need to apply methodologies that adopt predictive analytics and consumer-driven innovation to drive their product and service innovation, positioning, promotion, delivery and channel model, as well as overall customer engagement model, based on consumers' requests, interests, activities and attitudes as they occur and change in real time.

Technology is no longer a support function, but has become the key strategic component in business transformation and business model optimization and is a driver of the technology-enabled execution of the **BeProFit** transformational methodology.

Summary of Upcoming Cruising to Profits - Volume 2

- The Practical Guide -

Cruising to Profits - Volume 2 is the implementation and practical guide of the introductory book Cruising to Profits- Volume 1. It provides the practical content underpinning the vision and framework laid out in Ricardo Pilon's first airline management book.

Volume 2 appeals to (senior) airline management and aviation professionals who are interested in exploring how deep segmentation can allow travelers (or non-travelers) too build a concierge service around their own needs, all fulfilled through modern media channels such as social media.

Following years of debate on personalization and customization in air travel, Volume 2 demonstrates that this is possible as soon as we stop focusing on the flight portion of the trip. Further detail can be found on www.cruising2profits.com, www.cruisetoprofits.com or www.millavia.com.

Summary of Upcoming Cruising to Profits - Volume 3

- The Human Capital Factor -

Leadership and Management are two different things but they both have a relationship to a company's profitability in terms of the effective use of people, talent, and motivation. Besides transformational strategies with regards to business model life cycles and turnaround plans, another key factor in airline profitability is the human factor. Regardless of solid business models, people have a direct impact on the ability of a firm to generate sustainable profits from the delivery of its services or products.

In *Cruising to Profits - The Human Capital Factor*, new introduce management frameworks and methodologies are introduced which awake leadership and talents and can turn people into profitable change agents. Using case studies from past experiences, the book draws a direct link between human factors and returns on capital.

CRUISING TO PROFITS
Transformational Strategies for Sustained Airline Profitability

A number of proprietary techniques, such as the "Human Capital Multiplier Method" and "$H^2 = S.T.A.R.$" are presented in this second volume of the **Cruising to Profits** series. It builds on the practical business transformation methods that were described in this first volume as the "**BeProFit**" methodology. This methodology is supported by three proprietary tools and service products of which further detail can be found on www.cruising2profits.com, www.cruisetoprofits.com or www.millavia.com.

Cruising to Profits Toolkits

This book comes with a number of practical management tools to help you assess your airline's profitability performance and a framework for business transformation.

These tools are available for download on the dedicated portal www.cruisetoprofits.com/toolkits.

CRUISING TO PROFITS

Transformational Strategies for Sustained Airline Profitability

Additional Resources

All of the professional services we provide enable business transformation and commercial optimization through four sets of activities, **Speaking Engagements & Coaching**, **Value-Creation Facilitation**, **Tools & Training**, and **Free Educational Program.**

Details of our services can be found on:

http://www.millavia.com

The author can be contacted for free resources, free assistance and advisory as well as professional services at:

Ricardo Pilon:	rpilon@millavia.com
Phone:	+1 (800) 839-9046
Facebook:	www.facebook.com/cruising2profits
	www.facebook.com/millavia
Twitter:	@Cruise2Profits
	@millavia
	@rvpilon

CRUISING TO PROFITS

Transformational Strategies for Sustained Airline Profitability

Acknowledgements

My father ran a company in Curaçao, Netherlands Antilles for a large multinational conglomerate in The Netherlands in the 1970s and 1980s. I was nine years old when my father's boss came to visit us at home and asked me casually what I wanted to become later. I took my parents by surprise when I passionately stated my sense of purpose. I was going to change the face of aviation by running an airline business (then KLM). I was going to do it fundamentally differently.

I laid out a framework for how I would do it. Six years later I embarked on a rollercoaster, much like the one that typifies the airline industry.

So many people have crossed my path in 40 years. I have met thousands of people, notably in the last 10 years as I was helping thousands of individuals and over 200 companies through my consulting practice, active in all continents. All these people have had an influence on the person I am today and how I have evolved so far. I could not mention them all. But the experience has brought me back to that sense of purpose thanks to my wife Stephanie. I am profoundly grateful for the fact that she helped me in my own transformation.

There are two factors that drove this first book project. First, I have difficulty articulating why I am so passionate about the airline business; there are so many facets, but this is where I want to be. Second, I have learned that nothing fulfills me more profoundly than helping other individuals and communities grow, and facilitating airlines which connect people and cultures as well as economies to be successful.

I have invested a lot in myself and capitalized on dedication, willpower, and commitment. But other people have made the real difference and helped me follow through with this first book. I want to thank all of the people that have touched my life; specifically Stephanie for her support; my father for inspiring me to be entrepreneurial and showing me how to lead and be generous; my mother for all her support. I also want to thank my brothers Karel and Marcel for being a sounding board. I want to thank Dr. B. (Bryan Knight) for the encouragement to remove my personal obstacles, and Beverly Glazar for all her life-changing help. I also want to thank Allen and Jeannie for sticking with me. In addition I am thanking the academic institutions and my colleagues at Cranfield University, Concordia University, and Harvard University. I am also grateful to Kofi Sonokpon for having assisted me during the publication process. Finally, I thank Bernard Redondo for his friendship and insightful perspectives.

Boudewijn, rest in peace. I decided to complete this project after we met in Utrecht in April 2013. You will continue to change lives.

I dedicate this book to Stephanie, Ana-Sophia, and my parents.

—Ricardo V. Pilon
Montreal
January 2014

About Ricardo Vincent Pilon

With 19 years of practical airline management and management consulting experience at various organizational levels varying from line management to corporate management, Ricardo Pilon has worked in strategic planning, organization/governance, revenue management & pricing, alliances, marketing, distribution, network, and product planning in both passenger services and air cargo management.

He has worked for and consulted with over 210 airlines, air cargo operators, and other service companies. In recent years, Ricardo has been heavily involved in business transformation and innovation. He has served as a senior executive in medium and large companies as ad-interim management. His airline and management consulting days date back to employment with KPMG and a dozen international airlines and airline start-ups since 1990.

In 1995, Ricardo launched his own airline practice as **CEO** of **Millennium Aviation, Inc.** to pursue the application of his personal approach to airline management and help organizations transform themselves free from conventional thinking.

As a certified **IATA Facilitator**, Ricardo has also developed training courses for the International Air Transportation Association (IATA) and served part-time as **Adjunct Professor** at the International Aviation MBA at Concordia University in Montreal as well as at the Aviation MBA at B.U.A.A. University in Beijing, PRC between 2000 and 2008.

In 2014, Ricardo was also selected to lead and teach the Airline Management component of the inaugural Aviation Management Programme at **McGill University's School of Continued Education** in Montreal.

Ricardo is a regular speaker at international conferences and has led panels, roundtable discussions and has been a keynote speaker at over 40 events in 25 countries.

Having specialized in aviation management, Ricardo Pilon holds an **MBA in International Aviation** from Concordia University in Montreal, a **Master of Science in Air Transport Management** from Cranfield University in the United Kingdom, as well as a Bachelor of Science in International Management from the International Business School in the Netherlands.

Ricardo is also attending **Harvard Business School** at Harvard University in Cambridge, Mass., USA for the completion of the High Potentials Executive Leadership Program in 2014.

Ricardo now focuses on business transformation, business model optimization, strategic planning and management, profitability performance enhancement, leadership and talent-based startup companies. He also dedicates time and availability as a free resource to airlines, airports and governments that require help in growing local communities and economies in developing markets.

Ricardo is always available to connect, to exchange ideas and experiences.

Bibliography

AICPA, "Audits of Airlines", AICPA Industry Audit Guide, New York, NY, USA, 1999.

Air New Zealand, "We're Committed To Our Environment", corporate publication, Auckland, 2007.

Abeyratne, R.I.R., "Aviation Trends in the New Millennium", Ashgate, Burlington, VT, USA, 2001.

Amabile, T., Fisher, C.M., Pillemer, J., "IDEO's Culture of Helping, Harvard Business Review, January-February 2014 pp. 55-61.

Anthony, S.D., Johnson, W., Sinfield, J.V., & Altman, E.J., "The Innovator's Guide to Growth", Harvard Business Press, Boston, MA, USA, 2008.

Antoniou, A., "Economies of Scale in the Airline Industry – The Evidence Revisited", The Logistics and Transportation Review, Vol. 27, No. 2, June 1991, pp 159-184.

Barton, D., Wiseman, M., "Focusing Capital on the Long Term", Harvard Business Review, January-February 2014 pp. 45-52.

Barz, C., "Risk-Averse Capacity Control in Revenue Management", Springer Berlin Heidelberg, Germany, 2007.

Bazargan, M., "Airline Operations and Scheduling", Ashgate, Burlington, VT, USA, 2010.

Belobaba, P., Odoni, A., Barnhart, C., "The Global Airline Industry", Wiley, United Kingdom, 2009.

Berkun, S., "The Myths of Innovation", O'Reilly Media, Sebastopol, CA, USA, 2010.

Birkman, S., Capparell, S., "The Birkman Method", Jossey-Bass – A Wiley Brand, Danvers, MA, USA, 2013.

Bisignani, G., "Shaking the Skies", LID Publishing Ltd., London, United Kingdom, 2013.

Boatwright, P., Cagan, J., "Built to Love – Creating Products that Captivate Customers", Berrett-Koehler Publishers, Inc., San Francisco, USA, 2010.

Brueckner, J.K., "Economies of Traffic Density in the Deregulated Airline Industry", Journal of Law and Economics, Vol. 37, October 1994, pp. 379-391.

Burnison, G., "Lead", Korn/Ferry International, Danvers, MA, USA, 2013.

Calder, S., "No Frills – the truth behind the low-cost revolution in the skies", Virgin Books, United Kingdom, 2002.

Caes, D.W., Christensen, L.R., Tretheway, M.W., "Economies of density versus economies of scale", Rand Journal of Economics, Vol. 15 No. 4 Winter, 1984.

Chesbrough, H., "Open Business Models – How to Thrive in the New Inno-vation Landscape", Harvard Business School Press, Boston, MA, USA, 2006.

Chesbrough, H., "Open Innovation – The New Imperative For Creating and Profiting from Technology", Harvard Business School Press, MA, USA, 2006.

Clemmer, J., "Firing on all Cylinders", McGraw-Hill, New York, NY, USA, 1992.

Cokins, G., "Performance Management", John Wiley & Sons, New Jersey, USA, 2009.

Collins, J., "Good to Great", Harper Business, New York, NY, USA, 2001.

Collins, J., Hansen, M.T., "Great by Choice", Harper Business, New York, NY, USA, 2011.

Collins, J., "How the Might Fall", Harper Collins, New York, NY, USA, 2009.

Courtney, H., Loallo, D., Clarke, C., "Deciding How to Decide", Harvard Business Review, November 2013, pp. 63-70.

Cross, R.G., "Revenue Management – Hard Core Tactics for Market Domination", Broadway Books, New York, NY, 2007.

Dauphinais, W., Price, C., "Straight From The CEO", Nicholas Brealey Publishing Limited, London, UK, 1998.

Davenport, Th.H., Harris, J., "Competing on Analytics", Harvard Business School press, Boston, MA, USA, 2007.

Davenport, Th.H., Harris, J., & Morison, R., "Analytics at Work", Harvard Business School Publishing Corporation, Boston, MA, USA, 2010.

Dempsey, P.S., "Airport Planning & Development Handbook", McGraw-Hill, New York, USA, 2000.

Dempsey, P.S., Gesell, L.E., "Airline Management – Strategies for the 21st Century", Coast Aire Publications, Chandler, Arizona, USA, 1997.

Dieken, C., "Become The Real Deal", John Wiley & Sons, New Jersey, USA, 2013.

Dodson, R., "Unfriendly Skies", Doubleday, NY, 1989.

Doganis, R., "Flying off Course", Fourth Edition, Routledge, NY, 2010.

Doganis, R., "The Airport Business`, Routledge, NY, USA, 1992.

Downs, L., "The Laws of Disruption: Harnessing the New Forces that Govern Life and Business in the Digital Age", Basic Books, 2009.

Doz, Y., Kosonen, M., "Fast Strategy – How Strategic Agility will help you stay ahead of the Game", Wharton School Publishing, Harlow, United Kingdom, 2008.

Dixon, M., Toman, N., Delisi, R., "The Effortless Experience – Conquering The New Battleground For Customer Loyalty", Portfolio / Penguin, New York, NY, USA, 2013.

Dawar, N., "When Marketing IS Strategy", Harvard Business Review, December 2013, pp. 101-108.

Drucker, P.F., "Innovation and Entrepreneurship", Harper Collins Business, New York, NY, USA, 1993.

Edersheim, E.H., "McKinsey's Marvin Bower – Vision, Leadership & the Creation of Management Consulting", John Wiley & Sons, New Jersey, USA, 2004.

Farris, P., Bendle, N.T., Pfeifer, Ph.E., Reibstein, D.J., "Marketing Metrics", Wharton School Publishing, New Jersey, USA, 2006.

Faulkner, D., Bowman, C., "The Essence of Competitive Strategy", Prentice Hall, Hertfordshire, United Kingdom, 1995.

Fox., W.F., "International Commercial Agreements", Kluwer Publishers, Deventer, Netherlands, 1992.

Friga, P.N., "The McKinsey Engagement", McGraw-Hill, New York, NY, USA, 2009.

Gasdia, M., and Quinby, D., "The Captives are Capitulating", PhoCusWright, Inc., 2013.

George, M., Rowlands, D., & Kastle, B., "What is Lean Six Sigma?", McGraw-Hill, New York, NY, USA, 2004.

Gillen, D.W., "Airline Cost Structure and Policy Implications", Journal of Transport Economics and Policy, Vol. 24, No. 1, January 1999.

Godin, S., "Tribes – We Need You to Lead Us", Penguin Group, New York, NY, 2008.

Goleman, D., "Focus: the hidden driver of excellence", Harper Collins, New York, NY, 2013.

Goleman, D., "The Focused Leader", Harvard Business Review, December 2013, pp. 51-58.

Graham, D.R., Kaplan, D.P., Sibley D.S., "Efficiency and competition in the airline industry", BELL Journal of Economics, Vol. 14, No. 1, Spring 1983.

Hamel, G., "The Future of Management", Harvard Business School Press, Boston, MA, USA, 2007.

Hanlon, P., "Global Airlines – Competition in a Transnational Industry", Butterworth Heinemann, Oxford, United Kingdom, 1997.

Hansen, M.T., "Collaboration", Harvard Business Press, Boston, MA, USA, 2009.

Harmon, P., "Business Process Change", Morgan Kaufmann Publishers, San Francisco, CA, USA, 2003.

Harvard Business Review, "On Change", Harvard Business School Press, Boston, MA, USA, 2008.

Harvard Business Review, "Breakthrough Thinking", Harvard Business School Press, Boston, MA, USA, 1999.

Hellriegel, D., Slocum, J.W., Woodman, R.W., "Organizational Bahavior", West Publishing Company, St. Paul, MN, USA, 1992.

Hellermann, R., "Capacity Options for Revenue Management", Springer Berlin Heidelberg, Germany, 2006.

Henry, T., "The Accidental Creative", Portfolio/Penguin, New York, NY, 2011.

Hill, Ch.W.L., Jones, G.R., "Strategic Management", Houghton Mifflin Company, Boston, MA, USA, 1998.

Hippel, E. von., "Democratizing Innovation", MIT Press, Cambridge, MA, USA, 2005.

Hollaway, S., "Airlines – Managing to Make Money, Ashgate,

Hollins, S., "Back to mobile marketing basics", Beyond Analysis, 2013.

Hooser, Ph. Van., "Leaders Ought to Know", "John Wiley & Sons, New Jersey, USA, 2013.

Hoppe, E., "Ethical Issues in Aviation", Ashgate, Burlington, VT, USA, 2011.

Hutcheson, S., "An Introduction to Air Transportation", Aviation Training International, Australia, 1996.

Jong, D. de, Kaashoek, B., and Zondag, W-J., "Blue Skies or Storm Clouds – Essays on Public Policy & Air Transport", ScienceGuide, 2008.

Johns, G., "Organizational Behavior", Fourth Edition, Harper Collins, New York, NY, 1996.

Johnson, G., Scholes, K.,"Exploring Corporate Strategy", Fourth Edition, Prentice Hall, Hertfordshire, United Kingdom, 2007.

Kelton Global / Carlson Rezidor Hotel Group, www.carlsonrezidor.com, 2013.

Kim, W.C., Mauborgne, R., "Blue Ocean Strategy", Harvard Business School Press, Boston, MA, USA, 2005.

Kirby, M.G., "Airline Economics of Scale", Journal of Transport Economics, Vol. 30, No. 3, September 1986.

Koch, R., "The 80/20 Manager", Little, Brown and Company, New York, NY, USA, 2013.

Kotler, Ph., "Marketing Management", Millennium Edition, Prentice Hall, New Jersey, USA, 2000.

Kotter, J.P., "A Sense of Urgency", Harvard Business Press, Boston, MA, USA, 2008.

Kumbhakar, S.C., "A Reexamination of Returns to Scale, Density and Technical Progress in U.S. Airlines, Southern Economic Journal pp. 428-442, October 1990.

Lencioni, P., "The Four Obsessions of an Extraordinary Executive", Jossey-Bass, San Francisco, CA, USA, 2000.

Lovelock, Ch., Wright, L., "Principles of Service Marketing & Management", Prentice Hall, New Jersey, USA, 2002.

Macario, R., Van de Voorde, E., "Critical Issues in Air Transport Economics and Business", Routledge, Oxon, United Kingdom, 2011.

Man, A-P. de., "Organizing for Competitiveness", Eburon Publishers, Delft, Netherlands, 1996.

Martin, D., "Retailers fight fire with delivery & fulfilment", Maxymiser, July 2013.

Martin, R.L., "The Big Lie of Strategic Planning", Harvard Business Review, January-February 2014 pp. 79-84.

McGrath, R. Gunther, "Transient Advantage", Strategy for Turbulent Times, Harvard Business Review, pp. 62-70, Boston, MA, USA, June 2013.

McKinsey Quarterly, Number 1, 2006, McKinsey & Company, New York, NY, 2006.

McKinsey Quarterly, Number 2, 2006, McKinsey & Company, New York, NY, 2006.

McKinsey Quarterly, Number 3, 2006, McKinsey & Company, New York, NY, 2006.

McKinsey Quarterly, Number 4, 2006, McKinsey & Company, New York, NY, 2006.

McKinsey Quarterly, Special Edition – Serving the Chinese Consumer, McKinsey & Company, New York, NY, 2006.

McKinsey Quarterly, Number 1, 2007, McKinsey & Company, New York, NY, 2006.

Mintzberg, H., "The Rise and Fall of Strategic Planning", The Free Press, New York, 1994.

Mintzberg, H., "Managers Not MBAs", Berrett-Koehler Publishers, Inc., San Francisco, CA, USA, 2005.

Mintzberg, H., Ahlstrand, B., Lampel, J., "Strategy Bites Back", Pearson Prentice Hall, New Jersey, USA, 2005.

Morrell, P.S., "Airline Finance", Ashgate Publishing Ltd, Aldershot, Hants, United Kingdom, 1997.

Morrison, S.A., Winston, C., "The Evolution of the Airline Industry", The Brookings Institution, Washington, D.C., USA, 1995.

Müller-Bungart, M., "Revenue Management with Flexible Products", Springer Berlin Heidelberg, Germany, 2007.

Nagle, Th.T., Holden, R.D., "The Strategy and Tactics of Pricing", Prentice Hall Marketing Series, New Jersey, USA, 2002.

Nellis, J.G., Parker, D., "The Essence of Business Economics", Second Edition, Prentice Hall, Hertfordshire, United Kingdom, 1997.

Nunes, P.F., Downes, L., "Big Bang Disruption – The Innovator's Disaster", Accenture, Outlook, no. 2, 2013.

Nunes, P.F., Yardley, S., Spelman, M., "A New Path to Growth, How to stay a step ahead of changing consumer behavior", Accenture, Outlook, no. 2, 2013.

O'Connor, W.E., "An Introduction to Airline Economics", Praeger, Westport, CT, USA, 1995.

Parmar, R., Mackenzie, I., Cohn, D., Gann, D., "The New Patternss of Innovation", Harvard Business Review, January-February 2014 pp. 86-95.

Pels, E., "Airport Economics and Policy", Tinbergen Institute, Amsterdam, 2000.

Pennington, R., "Make Change Work", John Wiley & Sons, New Jersey, USA, 2013.

Petzinger, Th. Jr, "Hard Landing", Aurum Press Ltd, London, United Kingdom, 1995.

Pfeffer, J., "Competitive Advantage Through People", Harvard Business School Press, Boston, MA, USA, 1995.

Philipps, R.L, "Pricing and Revenue Optimization", Stanford Business Books, Stanford, CA, USA, 2005.

Piazolo, F., Felderere, M., "Innovation and Future of Enterprise Information Systems", Springer Heidelberg Berlin, Germany, 2013.

Pink, D.H., "Drive", Riverhead Books, Penguin Group, New York, NY, USA, 2009.

Pilarski, A., "Why Can't We Make Money in Aviation?", Ashgate, Burlington, VT, USA, 2007.

Poteet, L, Stone, M., "Plane Talk", Robert Davies, Buffalo, NY, USA, 1997.

Radnoti, G., "Profit Strategies for Air Transportation", McGraw-Hill, New York, USA, 2002.

Rasiel, E.M., "The McKinsey Way", McGraw-Hill, New York, NY, USA, 1999.

Rasiel, E.M., Friga, P.N., "the McKinsey Mind", McGraw-Hill, New York, NY, USA, 2002.

Rawwon, A., Duncan, E., Jones C., "The Truth About Customer Experience", Harvard Business School, September 2013, pp. 90-98

Raynor, M.E., "The Strategy Paradox", Currency Doubleday, New York, NY, USA, 2007.

Redman, T.C., "Data's Credibility Problem", Harvard Business Review, December 2013, pp. 84-88.

Rosenzweig, P., "What Makes Strategic Decisions Different", Harvard Business Review, November 2013, pp. 89-93.

Ross, J.W., "You May Not Need Big Data After All", Harvard Business Review, December 2013, pp. 90-98.

Ryall, M.D., "The New Dynamics of Competition", Harvard Business Review, January-February 2014 pp. 80-87.

Sarker, R.A., Newton, Ch.S., "Optimization Modelling", CRC Press, Boca Raton, FL, 2008.

Seamster, T., Kanki, B., "Aviation Information Management", Ashgate, Burlington, VT, USA, 2002.

Shackford, K.M., Shackford, J.E., "Charting a Wiser Course – How Aviation Can Address the Human Side of Change", The Mattford Group Press, Incline Village, Nevada, USA, 2003.

Shaw, S., "Airline Marketing & Management", Pitman Publishing, London, United Kingdom, 1990.

Shaw, S., "Airline Marketing & Management", Fourth Edition, Ashgate Publishing Ltd, Aldershot, Hants, United Kingdom, 1999.

Simon, H., Bilstein, F.F., Luby, F., "Manage For Profit – Not For Market Share", Harvard Business School Press, Boston, MA, 2006.

Skarzynski, P., Gibson, R., "Innovation To The Core", Harvard Business Press, Boston, MA, USA, 2008.

Skene, W., "Turbulence", Douglas & McIntyre, Vancouver, BC, Canada, 1994.

Skift, 1 August 2013, www.skift.com

Starks, E., "Plane Leadership", Lulu, San Francisco, CA, USA, 2010.

Stern, C.W., Stalk Jr., G., "Perspectives on Strategy", Boston Consulting Group, John Wiley & Sons, New York, NY, USA, 1998.

Stich, R., "The Real Unfriendly Skies – Saga of Corruption", Diablo Western Press, Inc., Reno, Nevada, USA, 1990.

Stewart, S., "Flying The Big Jets", Third Edition, Airlife Publishing Ltd., Shrewsbury, United Kingdom, 1992.

Tabrizi, B.N., "Rapid Transformation", Harvard Business School Press, Boston, MA, USA, 2007.

Taneja, N., "The Passenger Has Gone Digital and Mobile", Ashgate, Burlington, VT, USA, 2011.

Taneja, N., "Flying Ahead of the Airplan", Ashgate Publishing Company, USA, 2008.

Taneja, N., "Fasten Your Seatbelt – The Passenger is Flying the Plane", Ashgate, Burlington, VT, USA, 2005.

Taneja, N., "Airline Survival Kit – Breaking Out of the Zero Profit Game", Ashgate, Burlington, VT, USA, 2003.

The Loyalty Divide, published by Acxiom and Loyalty 360.

Thomas, R.J., "Building a Game-Changing Talent Strategy", Harvard Business Review, January-February 2014 pp. 63-68.

Thomson, L., "Creative Conspiracy", Harvard Business Press, Boston, MA, 2013.

Travel Weekly, July 30 – 2013, www.travelweekly.com

Transportation Research Board, "Entry and Competition in the U.S. Airline Industry", Washington, USA, 1999.

Wells, A.T., "Airport Planning & Management", McGraw-Hill, New York, USA, 1996.

Wells, A.T., "Air Transportation – A Management Perspective", Third Edition, Wadsworth Publishing Company, Belmont, CA, USA, 1994.

Wojahn, O.W., "Airline Networks", Peter Lang, Brussels, Belgium, 2001.

Yeoman, I., Ingold, A., "Yield Management", Cassell, London, United Kingdom, 1997.

Zee, Han van der (ed.), "Business transformation in a networked world", Nolan Norton & Co, Addison Wesley Longman, Netherlands, 1999.

Zeni, R.H., "Improved Forecast Accuracy in Airline Revenue Management by Unconstraining Demand Estimated from Censored Data", Dissertation.com, USA, 2001.

Zenger, T., "Strategy: The Unique Challenge", Harvard Business Review, December 2013, pp. 52-58.

End Notes

[i] *This flight, by the St. Petersburg-Tampa Airboat Line, was piloted by Tony Janus, and carried the first paying passenger, the former mayor of St. Petersburg. That first flight lasted 23 minutes and covered 21 miles (Air Transport World, June 2013).*

[ii] A case in point is Iberia, who by July 2013 was still burning over USD 2.2 million each day.

[iii] Walker, K., *Air Transport World* July 2013, pp. 7.

[iv] At the time of the completion of this publication, the average price per barrel of Brent crude oil for 2013 was expected to be around USD 108, compared to USD 112 in 2012 (atwonline, July 2013).

[v] IATA, July 2013.

[vi] IATA, Financial Forecast, December 2013.

[vii] Ever since the eurocrisis began in Greece and as it spread, Europe has been the big uncertainty and risk to the return of industry profitability.

[viii] IATA, Financial Forecast, December 2013.

[ix] Aircraft, Maintenance, Crew and Insurance.

[x] The first generation of regional jets, such as the Bombardier CRJ, will be faced out rapidly until 2020 in favor of Superjet, Mitsubishi Regional Jet, Bombardier's CSeries and other new entrants.

[xi] *Air Transport World, June 2013 (atwonline.com).*

[xii] Star Alliances is noted for its focus on exploiting synergies that large-scale, global collaboration and the development of joint IT solutions can produce.

[xiii] For instance, Ryanair is bring competition to Alitalia on the key domestic route of Milan and Rome.

[xiv] Airline Business, July 2013, pp. 21.

[xv] Samoa Air, a scheduled and charter airline connecting the Islands of Samoa, has begun this scheme. There are standard passenger weights and luggage fees which when combined translate into a currency-based charge per kilogram.

[xvi] By May 2013, an average of 5 percent of airline revenue world-wide consisted of ancillary revenue, and it has been on a steady rise, despite initial resistance from travelers. With the growth in value-added amenities and services associated with ancillary fees, travelers are now increasingly accustomed to this and perceive some as choice-based (premium) services. Some ancillary revenues, however, are still punitive in nature.

[xvii] Visiting Friends and Relatives.

[xviii] Air Canada introduced a piano bar on its Boeing 747 aircraft, although the experience represented significant challenges with regards to building the piano

on board, the time the aircraft were grounded for build-up as well as the realities of tuning requirements due to weather and humidity changes.

xix Including elements such as origins, destinations, itineraries, chosen amenities and paid-for preferences, and so forth.

xx Shifting Alliances, Air Transport World, July 2013, pp. 27

xxi Another example is that Qantas had to discontinue its longtime "Joint Service Agreement" (JSA) with fellow oneworld founding member British Airways so it could team up with Emirates, a surprising reversal of the latter's independent stance regarding alliances.

xxii *Source: t2social.com, 19 July 2013.*

xxiii *Angel, R. and Sexsmith, J. (2009), "Social Networking: The View from the C-Suite", Ivey Business Journal.*

xxiv This case study was published by Social Media Today in April 2013.

xxv Airline Business, July 2013, pp. 35.

xxvi *eMarketer, May 2013.*

xxvii The practice of increasing or decreasing the accessibility to seats at certain fare levels based on the market based on their willingness to pay.

xxviii The practice of discriminatory pricing through the use of restrictions or flexibility based on the needs of travelers as categorized by market segmentation.

xxix Airline Business, Airline IT Trends Survey results, Airline Business July 2013, pp. 28-29.

xxx Edutainment is a trend towards combining gaming, entertainment with educational content, aimed at providing younger generations with games that combine learning and education with juvenile fun.

www.ingramcontent.com/pod-product-compliance
Lightning Source LLC
Chambersburg PA
CBHW021827090426
42811CB00032B/2050/J